Great Americana

The World Encompassed

Sir Francis Drake

The World Encompassed
by Sir Francis Drake

READEX MICROPRINT

Foreword

The World Encompassed by Sir Francis Drake, published in London in 1628, a half century after the events that it chronicles, purports to be an official narrative of the first circumnavigation of the world by an Englishman. England and Spain were again at war, and the spirit of the great sea dog was to be invoked to fire his countrymen with some of Drake's own patriotic zeal.

"Ever since Almighty God commanded Adam to subdue the earth," runs the preamble, "there have not wanted in all ages some heroical spirits which, in obedience to that high mandate...have expended their wealth, employed their times, and adventured their persons to find out the true circuit thereof."

The first such heroical spirit to put a girdle about the globe was Ferdinand Magellan. The great Portuguese navigator, however, had died en route, leaving to Drake the distinction of being the first captain to take his ship the whole way. More significant is the claim made by some historians that the voyage of 1577-1580 was the first step toward the founding of the British Empire.

That empire-building was a conscious goal in the minds of Drake and the backers of his expedition, among them Queen Elizabeth I, may be doubted. The true objective of the undertaking, however, remains one of its several mysteries. Was it a search for the western end of the Northwest Passage to the Indies, the legendary Straits of Anian? Drake's push up the west coast to 42° or 43° N. latitude would seem to suggest it. Although he abandoned the search for the passage, he went on to load a cargo of spices in the Moluccas and to conclude trading agreements with the Sultan of Ternate. But if the wealth of the Indies was his ultimate goal, Drake did not overlook riches nearer at hand. In staking a claim to New Albion, in the San Francisco Bay region, for England, was he looking for territory "out of the jurisdiction of any Christian king" for a base of operations against the treasure trove of Spain's silver mines in Peru? Or was it enough that the "Golden Hind," so low in the water with loot taken along the way that she nearly foundered on a reef, brought a profit to her investors estimated as high as 4,700 per cent? Probably there were as many motives for the voyage as there were backers.

The name and auspices of Sir Francis Drake, nephew of the admiral, led to contemporary acceptance of *The World Encompassed* as an authorized version of the circumnavigation story. Actually it is a compilation "carefully collected [and edited] out of the notes of Master Francis Fletcher," chaplain on the voyage, "and divers others his followers in the same." One of the "divers others" was Richard Hakluyt, who first published an account of the circumnavigation in the second edition of his *Principal Navigations . . . of the English Nation* (1600).

A full account of the voyage and documentary sources can be found in *Sir Francis Drake's Voyage around the World* by Henry R. Wagner (San Francisco, 1926).

The World Encompassed

AVXILIO·DI·VINO

SIC·PARVIS·MAGNA

Drake pevorati novit quem terminus orbis
Et quem bis mundi vidit vtera Polus:
Si taceant homines, facient te Sidera notum,
Sol nescit comitis non memor esse sui.

THE VVORLD
Encompassed

By
Sir FRANCIS DRAKE,

Being his next voyage to that to *Nombre de Dios* formerly imprinted;

Carefully collected out of the notes of Master
FRANCIS FLETCHER *Preacher in this imployment, and diuers others his followers in the same*:

Offered now at last to publique view, both for the honour o
the actor, but especially for the stirring vp of *heroick spirits,
to benefit their Countrie, and eternize their names
by like noble attempts.*

LONDON,
Printed for NICHOLAS BOVRNE
and are to be sold at his shop at the
Royall Exchange. 1628.

WATER

EARTH

Mr Thomas Cavendish.

NORTH

Oliverus Vander Noort.

This South part of the World (conteyning almost the third part of the Globe) is yet vnknowne certayne sea coasts excepted: which rather shew there is a land then discry eyther land, people, or Comodities.

THE SOV THERNE VNKNO NE LAND

The Antarticke Circle

SOUTH

The Eclipse of the Moone

Ro: Vaughan fecit

TO
THE TRVLY NOBLE
R OBERT Earle of VVARVVICKE.

Right Honourable,

Ame and enuie are both
needleſſe to the dead becauſe
vnknowne, ſometimes dangerous to the liuing when too
well knowne: reaſon enough
that I rather chuſe to ſay no-
thing, then too little, in the praiſe of the decea-
ſed Author, or of your Lordſhip my deſired fau-
tor. Columbus *did neatly checke his* emula-
tors, *by rearing an egge without aſſiſtance.* Let
the ſlighter of this voyage applie. If your Lordſhip vouchſafe the acceptance, 'tis yours, if the

Reader

The Epistle

Reader can picke out either vse or content, tis his, and I am pleased. Example being the publique, and your Lordships fauor the priuate aime, of

Your humbly deuoted,

FRANCIS DRAKE.

THE VOYAGE ABOVT
the world, by Sir FRANCIS DRAKE.

Ver since Almighty God commanded *Adam* to fubdue the earth, there haue not wanted in all ages, fome heroicall fpirits, which in obedience to that high mandate, either from manifeft reafon alluring them, or by fecret inftinct inforcing them thereunto, haue expended their wealth, imployed their times, and aduentured their perfons, to finde out the true circuit thereof.

Of thefe, fome haue endeauored to effect this their purpofe, by conclufion and confequence, drawne from the proportion of the higher circles, to this nethermoft globe, being the center of the reft. Others not contented with fchoole points. and fuch demonftrations (for that a fmall errour in the beginning, groweth in the progreffe to a great inconuenience) haue added thereunto their owne hiftory and experience. All of them in reafon haue deferued great commendation of their owne ages, and purchafed a iuft renowne with all pofterity. For if a furueyer of fome few Lordfhips, whereof the bounds and limits were before knowne, worthily deferue his reward, not onely for his trauell, but for his skill alfo, in meafuring the whole and euerie part thereof: how much more, aboue comparifon, are their famous trauells by all meanes poffible to be eternized, who haue beftowed their ftudies and indeauor, to furuey and meafure this globe allmoft vnmeafurable? Neither is here that difference to be obiected

iected, which in priuate posseffions is of value: *whose Land suruey you?* forasmuch as the maine Ocean by right is the Lords alone, and by nature left free, for all men to deale withall, as very suffi-cient for all mens vse, and large enough for all mens induftry.

And therefore that valiant enterprife, accompanied with happy fucceffe, which that right rare and thrice worthy Cap-taine *Francis Drake* atcheiued, in firft turning vp a furrow about the whole world, doth not onely ouermatch the ancient Argo-nautes, but alfo outreacheth in many refpects, that noble mari-ner *Magellanus* and by farre furpaffeth his crowned victory. But hereof let pofterity iudge.

It fhall, for the prefent, be deemed a fufficient difcharge of duty, to regifter the true and whole hiftory of that his voyage, with as great indifferency of affection as a hiftory doth require, and with the plaine euidence of truth, as it was left recorded by fome of the chiefe, and diuers other actors in that action.

The faid Captaine *Francis Drake*, hauing in a former voy-age, in the yeares 72. and 73. (the defcription whereof is already imparted to the veiw of the world) had a fight, and onely a fight of the fouth Atlantik, and thereupon either conceiuing a new, or renewing a former defire, of failing on the fame, in an Englifh bottom; he fo cherifhed thenceforward, this his noble defire and refolution in himfelfe, that notwithftanding he was hinde-red for fome yeares, partly by fecret enuie at home, and partly by publique feruice for his Prince and countrie abroad, (wherof Ireland vnder Walter Earle of Effex giues honorable teftimonie) yet, againft the yeare 1577. by gratious commiffion from his foueraigne, and with the helpe of diuers friends ad-uenturers, he had fitted himfelfe with fiue fhips.

1. *The Pellican.* admirall. burthen 100. tonnes. Captaine generall. *Francis Drake.*

2. *The Elizabeth.* vice admirall. burthen 80. tonnes. Cap-taine *Iohn Winter.*

3. *The Marigold.* a bark of 30. tonnes. Captaine *Iohn Thomas.*

4. *The Swanne.* a fliboat of 50. tonnes. Captaine *Iohn Chefter.*

5. *The*

5. *The Chriſtopher,* a pinnace of 15. tonnes. Captaine *Tho-*
mas Moone.

Theſe ſhips he mand with 164. able and ſufficient men, and
furniſhed them alſo with ſuch plentifull prouiſion of all things
neceſſary, as ſo long and dangerous a voyage did ſeeme to require: and amongſt the reſt, with certaine pinnaces ready fra-
med, but caried aboard in peices, to be new ſet vp in ſmoother
water, when occaſion ſerued. Neither had he omitted, to make
prouiſion alſo for ornament and delight, carying to this purpoſe
with him, expert muſitians, rich furniture (all the veſſels for his
table, yea many belonging euen to the Cooke-roome being
of pure ſiluer) and diuers ſhewes of all ſorts of curious workmanſhip, whereby the ciuilitie and magnificence of his natiue contrie, might, amongſt all nations whitherſoeuer he ſhould come,
be the more admired.

Being thus appointed we ſet ſaile out of the ſound of Plimmouth, about 5. of the clocke in the afternoone Nouember
15. of the ſame yeare, and running all that night Southweſt, by
the morning were come as farre as the Lyzard, where meeting
the winde at Southweſt (quite contrarie to our intended courſe)
we were forced, with our whole fleet to put in to Falmouth.

The next day, towards euening, there aroſe a ſtorme, continuing all that night, and the day following (eſpecially betweene
10. of the clocke in the forenoone, and 5. in the after noone)
with ſuch violence, that though it were in a verygood harbor,
yet 2. of our ſhips viz. the admirall (wherein our generall himſelfe went) and the Marigold, were faine to cut their maine maſts
by board, and for the repairing of them, and many other dam-
mages in the tempeſt ſuſtained (as ſoone as the weather would
giue leaue) to beare backe to Plimmouth againe, where wee all
arriued the 13. day after our firſt departure thence.

Whence (hauing in few daies ſupplied all defects) with hap-
pier ſayles we once more put to ſea *December* 13. 1577.

As ſoone as we were out of ſight of land, our generall gaue
vs occaſion to coniecture in part, whither he intended, both by
the

the directing of his courſe, and appointing the *Randevous* (if
any ſhould bee ſeuered from the fleet) to be the Iland, *Mo-*
gadore. And ſo ſailing with fauorable windes, the firſt land that
wee had ſight of, was *Cape Cantine* in *Barbarie December* 25.
Chriſtmas day in the morning. The ſhoare is faire white ſand,
and the inland contrie very high and mountainous, it lieth in
32. deg. 30. mi. north latitude, and ſo coaſting from hence
ſouthward, about 18. leagues, we arriued the ſame day at
Mogadore the Iland before named.

This *Mogadore*, lies vnder the dominion of the king of *Feſſe* in
31. deg. 40. mi. about a mile off from the ſhoare, by this meanes
making a good harbor betweene the land and it. It is vninhabi-
ted, of about a league in circuit, not very high land, all ouergrowne with a kinde of ſhrub breſt high, not much vnlike our
priuet, verie full of Doues and therefore much frequented of
Goſhaukes, and ſuch like birds of prey, beſides diuers ſorts of
ſea-foule very plentie. At the ſouth ſide of this Iland are three
hollow rocks, vnder which are great ſtore of very wholeſome
but very vglie fiſh to looke to. Lying here about a mile from
the maine, a boate was ſent to ſound the harbor, and finding it
ſafe, and in the very entrance on the north ſide about 5. or 6.
fathome water (but at the ſouther ſide it is very dangerous) we
brought in our whole fleet *December* 27. and continued there
till the laſt day of the ſame moneth, imploying our leaſure, the
meane while, in ſetting vp a pinnace, one of the 4. brought from
home in peices with vs. Our abode here was ſoone perceiued by
the inhabitants of the contrie, who comming to the ſhoare, by
ſignes and cries made ſhewe, that they deſired to be fetched a-
board, to whom our generall ſent a boate, into which 2. of the
chiefeſt of the *Moores* were preſently receiued, and one man
of ours, in exchange, left a land, as a pledge for their returne.

They that came aboard were right courteouſly entertained,
with a daintie banquet, and ſuch gifts as they ſeemed to be moſt
glad of, that they might thereby vnderſtand, that this fleete
came in peace and friendſhip, offering to traffique with them,

for

for such commodities as their contrie yeelded, to their owne content. This offer they seemed most gladly to accept, and promised, the next day, to resort againe, with such things as they had to exchange for ours. It is a law amongst them to drinke no wine, notwithstanding by stealth it pleaseth them well to haue it abundantly, as here was experience. At their returne ashoare, they quietly restored the pledge which they had stayed, and the next day, at the houre appointed, returning againe, brought with them Camells, in shewe loaden with wares to be exchanged for our commodities, and calling for a boate in haste, had one sent them, according to order, which our generall(being at this present absent)had giuen before his departure to the Iland.

Our boate comming to the place of landing(which was among the rocks) one of our men called *Iohn Fry*, mistrusting no danger, nor fearing any harme pretended by them, and therefore intending to become a pledge, according to the order vsed the day before, readilie stept out of the boate and ranne a land, which oportunitie(being that which the *Moores* did looke for) they tooke the aduantage of, and not onely they which were in sight, layed hands on him to carrie him away with them, but a number more, which lay secretly hidden, did forthwith breake forth from behinde the rocks, whither they had conueyed themselues (as it seemeth the night before) forcing our men to leaue the rescuing of him that was taken as captiue, and with speed to shift for themselues.

The cause of this violence, was a desire which the king of *Fesse* had, to vnderstand what this fleet was, whether any forerunner of the kings of *Portugall* or no, and what newes of certaintie the fleet might giue him. And therefore after that he was brought to the kings presence, and had reported that they were Englishmen, bound for the straights, vnder the conduct of generall *Drake*, he was sent back againe with a present to his Captaine and offer of great curtesie and freindship, if he would vse his contry. But in this meane time, the generall being grieued with this shew of iniurie, and intending, if he might, to recouer or redeeme his man, his pinnace being ready, landed his company, and marched somewhat into the countrie, without any resistance made against him: neither would the *Moores*, by any meanes come nigh our men, to deale with them any way; wherefore hauing made prouision of wood, as also visited an old fort, built sometime by the king of *Portugall*, but now ruined by

the king of *Fesse*, we departed *December* 31. towards *Cape Blanck*, in such sort, that when *Fry* returned, he found to his great griefe, that the fleet was gone: but yet, by the kings fauor, he was sent home into *England* not long after, in an English Marchants ship.

Shortly after our putting forth of this harbour, we were met with contrary windes and foule weather, which continued till the fourth of Ianuary: yet we still held on our course, and the

third day after, fell with cape *De Guerre* in 30. deg. min. where wee lighted on 3. Spanish fishermen called *Caunters*, whom we tooke with our new pinnace, and caried along with vs, till

we came to *Rio Del Oro*, iust vnder the Tropick of Cancer: where with our pinnace also we took a caruell. From hence, till

the fifteenth day, we sailed on towards cape *Barbas*, where the Marigold tooke a caruell more, and so onward to cape *Blanck*

till the next day at night.

This cape lieth in 20. deg. 30. min. shewing it selfe vpright like the corner of a wall, to them that come towards it from the North, hauing, betweene it and cape *Barbas*, lowe, sandy, and very white land all the way. Here we obserued the south *Guards*, called the *Crosiers* 9. deg. 30. min. aboue the horizon. Within the cape, we tooke one spanish ship more riding at anchor (all her men being fled ashoare in the boate saue two) which, with all the rest we had formerly taken, we caried into the harbor, 3. leagues within the cape.

Here our generall determined, for certaine dayes to make his abode, both for that the place afforded plenty of fresh victualls, for the present refreshing of our men, and for their future supply at sea (by reason of the infinite store of diuers sorts of

good

good fiſh, which are there eaſie to be taken, euen within the
harbor, the like whereof, is hardly to be found againe, in any
part of the world) as alſo, becauſe it ſerued very fitly, for the diſ-
patching of ſome other buſineſſes that we had. During the time
of our abode in this place, our generall being aſhoare was viſited by certaine of the people of the country, who brought
downe with them a woman a *Moore* (with her little babe hanging vpon her dry dugge, hauing ſcarce life in herſelfe, much
leſſe milke to nouriſh her child) to be ſould as a horſe, or a cow
and calfe by her ſide, in which ſort of merchandiſe our generall
would not deale. But they had alſo Amber-greece, with certaine gummes of ſome eſtimation, which they brought to exchange with our men for water (whereof they haue great want)
ſo that comming with their *Allforges* (they are leathern bags
holding liquor) to buy water, they cared not at what price they
bought it, ſo they might haue to quench their thirſt. A very heauie iudgement of God vpon that coaſt! The circumſtances
whereof conſidered, our generall would receiue nothing of
them for water, but freely gaue it them that came to him, yea
and fed them alſo ordinarily with our victualls, in eating whereof, their manner was not onely vnciuill, and vnſightly to vs, but
euen inhumane and loathſome in it ſelfe.

And hauing waſhed and trimd our ſhips, and diſcharged all
our ſpaniſh priſes, excepting one *Caunter* (for which we gaue to
the owner one of our owne ſhips viz. the Chriſtopher) and one
caruell formerly bound to Saint *Iago,* which we cauſed to acom-
panie vs hither, where ſhee alſo was diſcharged: after 6. dayes
abode here, we departed, directing our courſe for the Ilands of ***Ian. 22.***
cape *Verde,* where (if any where) we were of neceſſity to ſtore
our fleet with freſh water, for a long time, for that our generall
intended from thence, to runne a long courſe (euen to the coaſt
of *Braſill*) without touch of land. And now, hauing the winde
conſtant at *North Eaſt & Eaſt North Eaſt,* which is vſuall about
thoſe parts, becauſe it bloweth almoſt continually from the
ſhoare. *Ianuary* the 27. we coaſted *Bonaviſta,* and the next day

after, we came to anchor vnder the VVester part (towards Saint *Iago*) of the Iland *Maio*, it lyeth in 15 deg. 00. high land, sauing that the North west part stretcheth out into the sea, the space of a league very low, and is inhabited by subiects to the king of Portugall.

Here landing, in hope of traffique with the inhabitants for water, we found a Towne, not farre from the waters side, of a great number of desolate and ruinous houses, with a poore naked Chappell or Oratory, such as small cost and charge might serue and suffice, being to small purpose, and as it seemeth onely to make a shew, and that a false shew, contrary to the nature of a scarcrow, which feareth birds from comming nigh; this entiseth such as passe by, to hale in, and looke for commodity, which is not at all to be found there; though in the inner parts of the Iland it be in great abundance.

For when wee found the springs and wells which had beene there (as appeared) stopped vp againe, and no other water, to purpose, to bee had to serue our need, we marched vp to seeke some more conuenient place to supply our want, or at least to see whether the people would be dealt withal, to helpe vs therein. In this trauelling, we found the soile to be very fruitfull, hauing euery where plenty of figgetrees, with fruite vpon most of them. But in the vallies and low ground, where little low cottages were built, were pleasant vineyards planted, bearing then, ripe and most pleasant grapes. There were also tall trees, without any branch till the top, which bare the *Coco nuts.* There were also great store of certaine lower trees, with long and broad leaues, bearing the fruit which they call *Plantanes*, in clusters together like puddings, a most dainty and wholesome fruit. All of these trees were euen laden with fruit, some ready to be eaten, others comming forward, others ouer-ripe. Neither can this seeme strange, though about the middest of Winter with vs for that the Sunne doth neuer withdraw himselfe farther off from them, but that with his liuely heate he quickeneth and strengtheneth the power of the soyle and plant; neither euer haue they

any

any such frost and cold, as thereby to loose their greene hew and appearance.

We found very good water in diuerse places, but so farre off from the roade, that wee could not with any reasonable paines enioy it. The people would by no meanes be induced to haue any conference with vs, but keeping in the most sweet and fruit-full vallies among the hils, where their townes and places of dwelling were, gaue vs leaue without interruption to take our pleasure in suruewing the Iland, as they had some reason, not to endanger themselues, where they saw they could reape nothing sooner then damage and shame, if they should haue offered vio-lence to them which came in peace to do them no wrong at all.

This Iland yeeldeth other great commodities, as wonderfull heards of goats, infinite store of wilde hens, and salt without la-bour (onely the gathering it together excepted) which conti-nually in a maruellous quantitie is increased vpon the sands by the flowing of the sea, and the heate of the Sunne kerning the same. So that of the increase thereof they keepe a continuall traf-fique with their neighbours in the other adiacent Ilands. Wee set sayle thence the 30. day.

Being departed from *Maio*, the next day wee passed by the Iland of Saint *Iago*, ten leagues West of *Maio* in the same lati-tude, inhabited by the Portugals and Moores together. The cause whereof is said to haue beene in the Portugals themselues, who (continuing long time Lords within themselues, in the said Iland) vsed that extreame and vnreasonable crueltie ouer their slaues, that (their bondage being intollerable) they were forced to seeke some meanes to helpe themselues, and to lighten that so heauy a burden; and thereupon chose to flie into the most mountany parts of the Iland: and at last, by continuall escapes, increasing to a great number, and growing to a set strength, do now liue, with that terror to their oppressors, that they now endure no lesse bondage in mind then the *Portugals* did before in body: besides the dammage that they daily suffer at their hands in their goods and cattell, together with the abrid-

B 3 ging

ging of their liberties in the vſe of diuerſe parts of the fruitfull ſoile of the ſaid Iland: which is very large, maruellous fruitfull (a refuge for all ſuch ſhips as are bound towards Braſill, Ginny, the Eaſt Indies, Binny, Calecut. &c.) and a place of rare force, if it were not for the cauſe afore-recited, which hath much abated the pride, and cooled the courage of that people, who (vnder pretence of traffique and friendſhip) at firſt making an entrance ceaſed not, practiſing vpon the poore Ilanders (the ancient remainder of the firſt planters thereof, as it may ſeeme from the coaſt of Guinea) vntil they had excluded them from all gouernment and liberty, yea almoſt life.

On the South-weſt of this Iland, we tooke a Portugall laden the beſt part with wine, and much good cloth, both linnen and woollen, beſides other neceſſaries, bound for Braſill, with many gentlemen and Marchants in her.

As we paſſed by with our fleet, in ſight of 3. of their townes, they ſeemed very ioyfull that wee touched not with their coaſt; and ſeeing vs depart peaceably, in honour of our fleet and Generall, or rather to ſignifie that they were prouided for an aſſault, ſhot off two great peeces into the ſea, which were anſwered by one giuen them againe from vs.

South-weſt from Saint *Iago* in 14. deg. 30. min. about twelue leagues diſtant, yet, by reaſon of the height ſeeming not aboue three leagues lyeth another Iland, called of the Portugals *Fogo*, viz. the burning Iland, or fierie fornace, in which riſeth a ſteepe vpright hill, by coniecture at leaſt ſix leagues, or eighteene Engliſh miles from the vpper part of the water: within the bowels whereof, is a conſuming fire, maintained by ſulphury matter, ſeeming to be of a maruellous depth, and alſo very wide. The fire ſheweth it ſelfe but foure times in an houre, at which times it breaketh out with ſuch violence and force, and in ſuch maine abundance, that beſides that it giueth light like the Moone a great way off, it ſeemeth, that it would not ſtay till it touch the heauens themſelues. Herein are ingendred great ſtore of pumice ſtones, which being in the vehement heate of the fire caried vp

without

without the mouth of that fiery body, fall downe, with other grosse and slimy matter vpon the hill, to the continuall increasing of the same. And many times these stones falling downe into the sea are taken vp and vsed, as we our selues had experience by sight of them swimming on the water. The rest of the Iland is fruitfull notwithstanding, and is inhabited by Portugals, who liue very commodiously therein, as in the other Ilands thereabout.

Vpon the South side, about two leagues off this Iland of burning, lyeth a most sweet and pleasant Iland, the trees thereof are alwaies greene and faire to looke on, the soile almost full set with trees, in respect wherof its named the Braue Iland, being a storehouse of many fruits and commodities, as figges alwayes ripe, cocos, plantons, orenges, limons, cotton, &c. from the bancks into the sea do runne in many places the siluer streames of sweet and wholsome water, which with boats or pinnaces may easily be taken in. But there is no conuenient place or roade for ships, neither any anchoring at all. For after long triall, and often casting of leades, there could no ground be had at any hand, neither was it euer knowne (as is reported) that any line would fetch ground in any place about that Iland. So that the top of *Fogo* burneth not so high in the aire, but the roote of *Braua* (so is the Iland called) is buried and quenched as low in the seas.

The onely inhabitant of this Iland is an Heremit, as we suppose, for we found no other houses but one, built as it seemed for such a purpose; and he was so delighted in his solitarie liuing, that he would by no meanes abide our comming, but fled, leauing behind him the relicks of his false worship; to wit, a crosse, with a crucifix, an altar with his superaltar, and certaine other idols of wood of rude workemanship.

Here we dismissed the Portugals taken neere Saint *Iago*, and gaue to them in exchange of their old ship, our new pinnace built at Mogadore: with wine, bread, and fish for their prouision, *Feb.* 1. and so sent them away, Febr. 1.

Hauing thus visited, as is declared, the Ilands of cape *Verde*, and

1577.
Feb. 2.

Feb. 17.

Apr. 5.

and prouided fresh water as we could, the second of *Febr.* we departed thence, directing our course towards the straights, so to passe into the South sea, in which course wee sayled 63. dayes without sight of land (passing the line equinoctiall the 17. day of the same moneth) till we fell with the coast of Brasill, the fift of *April* following.

During which long passage on the vast gulph, where nothing but sea beneath vs and aire aboue vs was to be seene, as our eies did behold the wonderfull workes of God in his creatures, which he hath made innumerable both small and great beasts, in the great and wide seas : so did our mouthes taste, and our natures feed on, the goodnesse thereof in such fulnesse at all times, and in euery place, as if he had commanded and enioyned the most profitable and glorious works of his hands to waite vpon vs, not alone for the reliefe of our necessities, but also to giue vs delight in the contemplation of his excellence, in beholding the variety and order of his prouidence, with a particular tast of his fatherly care ouer vs all the while.

The truth is, wee often met with aduerse winds, vnwelcome stormes, and to vs (at that time) lesse welcome calmes, and being as it were in the bosome of the burning zone, we felt the effects of sultring heat, not without the affrights of flashing lightnings, and terrifyings of often claps of thunder; yet stil with the admixture of many comforts. For this we could not but take notice of, that whereas we were but badly furnished (our case considered) of fresh water (hauing neuer at all watred (to any purpose, or that we could say wee were much the better for it) from our first setting forth out of England till this time, nor meeting with any place where we might conueniently water, till our comming to the riuer of Plate, long after) continually, after once we were come within foure degrees of the line on this side, viz. after *Feb.* 10. and till we were past the line as many degrees towards the South, viz. till *Feb.* 27. there was no one day went ouer vs but we receiued some raine, whereby our want of water was much supplyed.

This

This also was obseruable, that of our whole fleet, being now 6. in number, notwithstanding the vncouthnes of the way, and what euer other difficulties, by weather or otherwise wee met withall, not any one, in all this space, lost company of the rest; except onely our Portugall prise for one day, who *March* 28. was seuered from vs, but the day following *March* 29. shee found vs againe, to both her owne, and our no little comfort : shee had in her 28. of our men, and the best part of all our prouision for drinke; her short absence caused much doubting and sorrow in the whole companie, neither could shee then haue been finally lost, without the ouerthrow of the whole voyage.

Among the many strange creatures which we sawe, we tooke heedfull notice of one, as strange as any ; to wit, the flying fish, a fish of the bignes and proportion, of a reasonable or middle sort of Pilchards : hee hath finnes, of the length of his whole body, from the bulk to the top of the taile, bearing the forme, and supplying the like vse to him, that wings doe to other creatures. By the helpe of these finnes, whē he is chased of the *Bonito*, or great mackrel(whom the *Aurata* or dolphin likewise pursueth) and hath not strength to escape by swimming any longer, hee lifteth vp himselfe aboue the water, and flieth a pretty height, sometimes lighting into boates or barkes as they saile along: The quills of their wings are so proportionable, and finelie set together, with a most thinne and dainty filme, that they might seeme to serue, for a much longer and higher flight, but the drienes of them is such, after some 10. or 12. strokes, that hee must needs into the water againe to moisten them, which else would grow stiffe and vnfit for motion. The increase of this little and wonderfull creature is in a manner infinite, the fry whereof lieth vpon the vpper part of the waters, in the heate of the Sun, as dust vpon the face of the earth, which being in bignesse of a wheat straw, and in length an inch more or lesse, do continually exercise themselues in both their faculties of nature : wherein, if the Lord had not made them expert indeed, their generation could not haue continued, being so desired a prey to so many,

C

which

which greedily hunt after them, forcing them to escape in the ayre by flight, when they cannot in the waters liue in safety. Neither are they allwayes free, or without danger, in their flying; but as they escape one euill, by refusing the waters, so they sometimes, fall into as great a mischiefe, by mounting vp into the ayre, and that, by meanes of a great and rauening foule, named of some a *Don* or *Spurkite,* who feeding chiefely, on such fish as he can come by at aduantage, in their swimming in the brim of the waters, or leaping aboue the same, presently ceaseth vpon them with great violence, making great havock, especially amongst these flying fishes, though with small profit to himselfe.

There is another sort of fish, which likewise flieth in the ayre, named a *Cuttill*: its the same, whose bones the goldsmithes commonly vse, or at least not vnlike that sort, a multitude of which, haue at one time, in their flight, fallen into our ships, amongst our men.

Passing thus, in beholding the most excellent works of the eternall God in the seas, as if we had beene in a garden of pleasure. Aprill 5. we fell with the coast of Brasill, in 3 1.deg. 30. min.

April 5. towards the pole Antartick, where the land is lowe neere the sea; but much higher within the countrie; hauing in depth not aboue 12. fathome, 3. leagues off from the shoare : and being descried by the inhabitants, we sawe great and huge fires, made by them in sundry plaes. Which order of making fires, though it be vniuersall, as well among Christians as heathens, yet is it not likely that many doe vse it to that end, which the Brasilians doe : to wit, for a sacrifice to Deuills, whereat they intermixe many and diuers ceremonies of coniurations, casting vp great heapes of sand, to this end, that if any ships, shall go about to stay vpon their coasts, their ministring spirits may make wrack of them, whereof the Portugalls by the losse of diuers of their ships, haue had often experience.

In the reports of Magellanes voyage, it is said, that this people pray to no maner of thing, but liue only according to the instinct of nature, which if it were true, there should seeme to be a

wonder-

wonderfull alteration in them, since that time, being fallen from
a simple and naturall creature, to make Gods of Deuills; But
I am of the minde, that it was with them then, as now it is, onely they lacked then the like occasion, to put it in practise which
now they haue: for then, they liued as a free people among
themselues, but now, are in most miserable bondage and slauery,
both in body, goods, wife, and children, and life it selfe to the
Portugalls, whose hard and most cruell dealings against them,
forceth them to flie, into the more vnfruitful parts of their owne
land, rather there to starue, or at least liue miserably with libertie, then to abide such intollerable bondage, as they lay vpon
them vsing the aforesaid practises with deuills, both for a reuenge against their oppressors, and also for a defence, that they
haue no further entrance into the country. And supposing indeed, that no other had vsed trauell by sea in ships, but their
enemies onely, they therefore vsed the same at our comming:
notwitstanding, our God made their deuilish intent of none effect; For albeit there lacked not (within the space of our falling
with this coast) forcible stormes and tempests, yet did we sust-
aine no dammage, but onely the seperating of our ships, out of
sight for a few dayes. Here our generall would haue gone a-
shore, but we could finde no harbor in many leagues. And
therefore coasting along the land, towards the south, Aprill 7.
we had a violent storme, for the space of 3. houres, with thunder, lightning, and raine in great abundance, accompanied
with a vehement south winde, directly against vs, which caused a seperation of the *Christopher* (viz. the Caunter which wee
tooke at cape *Blanck*, in exchange for the *Christopher*, whose
name she henceforward bore) from the rest of the fleet.

Apr. 7.

After this, we kept on our course, sometime to the sea ward,
sometimes toward the shoare, but alwayes southward, as neere
as we could: till Aprill 14. in the morning, at which time wee
passed by cape *Saint Mary*, which lies in 35. deg. neere
the mouth of the riuer of Plate: and running within it about 6.
or 7. leagues along by the maine, we came to anchor in a bay,

Apr. 14.

C 2   vnder

vnder another cape which our Generall afterwards called cape *Ioy*, by reason that the second day after our anchoring here, the Christopher (whom we had lost in the former storme) came to vs againe.

Among other cares which our Generall tooke in this action, next the maine care of effecting the voyage it selfe, these were the principall and chiefly subordinate: to keepe our whole fleet (as neere as possible we could) together; to get fresh water which is of continuall vse; and to refresh our men wearied with long toyles at sea, as oft as we should find any opportunitie of effecting the same. And for these causes it was determined, and publique notice thereof giuen at our departure from the Ilands of cape *Verde*; that the next Randeuous both for the recollecting of our nauy (if it should be desperfed) as also for watering, and the like, should be the riuer of Plate: whither we were all to repaire with all the conuenient speed that could be made, and to stay one for another, if it should happen that we could not arriue there all together; and the effect wee found answerable to our expectations, for here our seuered ship (as hath beene declared) found vs againe, and here we found those other helps also so much desired. The countrey hereabout is of a temperate and most sweet aire, very faire and pleasant to behold, and besides the exceeding fruitfulnesse of the soile, its stored with plentie of large and mightie deere.

Notwithstanding that in this first bay wee found sweet and wholsome water euen at pleasure; yet the same day after the arriuall of the Caunter, we remoued some twelue leagues farther vp into another; where we found a long rocke, or rather Iland of rocks, not farre from the maine; making a commodious harbor, especially against a Southerly wind: vnder them we anchored, and rode till the 20. day at night; in which meane space we killed diuers Seales, or sea-wolues (as the Spaniard cals them) which resorted to these rocks in great abundance. They are good meat, and were an acceptable food to vs for the present, and a good supply of our prouision for the future.

Hence

Hence *April* 20. we waighed againe and fayled yet further vp into the riuer, euen till we found but three fadome depth, and that we roade with our ſhips in freſh water ; but wee ſtaid not there, nor in any other place of the riuer, becauſe that the winds being ſtrong, the ſhoales many, and no ſafe harbour found, we could not without our great danger ſo haue done. Haling therefore to ſeaward againe, the 27. of the ſame moneth (after that we had ſpent a iuſt fortnight in that riuer, to the great comfort of the whole fleet) we paſſed by the South ſide thereof into the maine. The land here lieth South, South-weſt, and North N.E. with ſhole water, ſome three or foure leagues off into the ſea: its about 36. deg. 20. min. and ſomewhat better South latitude.

At our very firſt comming forth to ſea againe, to wit, the ſame night our flyboate the Swanne loſt company of vs: whereupon, though our Generall doubted nothing of her happy comming forward againe to the reſt of the fleete; yet becauſe it was grieuous to haue ſuch often loſſes, and that it was his duty as much as in him lay, to preuent all inconueniences beſides, that might grow; he determined to diminiſh the number of his ſhips, thereby to draw his men into leſſe roome; that both the fewer ſhips might the better keepe company, and that they might alſo bee the better appointed with new and freſh ſupplies of prouiſion and men, one to eaſe the burthen of another: eſpecially, for that he ſaw the coaſt (it drawing now toward Winter here) to bee ſubieſt to many and grieuous ſtormes : And therefore he continued on his courſe, to find out a conuenient harbour for that vſe; ſearching all that coaſt from 36. to 47. degrees (as diligently as contrary winds and ſundry ſtormes would permit) and yet found none for the purpoſe. And in the mean time viz. *May* 8. by another ſtorme the Caunter alſo was once more ſeuered frō vs.

May 12. wee had ſight of land, in 47. deg. where wee were forced to come to anchor in ſuch roade as we could find for the time. Neuertheleſſe our Generall named the place cape *Hope*, by reaſon of a bay diſcouered within the hedland, which ſeemed to promiſe a good and commodious harbour. But by reaſon of

C 3   many

many rockes lying off from the place, wee durſt not aduenture with our ſhips into it without good and perfect diſcouery before hand made.

Our Generall, eſpecially in matters of moment, was neuer wont to relye onely on other mens care, how truſty or skilfull ſoeuer they might ſeeme to be; but alwayes contemning danger and refuſing no toyle, he was wont himſelfe to be one whoſoeuer was a ſecond at euery turne, where courage, skill, or induſtry was to be imployed; neither would hee at this time intruſt the diſcouery of theſe dangers to anothers paines, but rather to his owne experience in ſearching out and ſounding of them. A boat being therefore hoiſed forth, himſelfe with ſome others the next *May* 13. morning, *May* 13. rowed into the bay; and being now very nigh the ſhore, one of the men of the countrey ſhewed himſelfe vnto him ſeeming very pleaſant, ſinging and dancing, after the noiſe of a rattle which he ſhooke in his hand, expecting earneſtly his landing.

But there was ſudainly ſo great an alteration in the weather, into a thick and miſty fogge; together with an extreame ſtorme and tempeſt, that our generall, being now 3. leagues from his ſhip, thought it better to returne, then either to land, or make any other ſtay: and yet the fogg thickened ſo mightily, that the ſight of the ſhips was bereft them, and if Captaine Thomas (vpon the abundance of his loue and ſeruice to his generall) had not aduentured, with his ſhip to enter that bay, in this perplexitie, where good aduiſe would not ſuffer our ſhips to beare in, while the windes were more tolerable, and the ayre cleerer; we had ſuſtained ſome great loſſe, or our generall had beene further endangered, who was now quickly receiued abord his ſhip; out of which, being within the bay, they let fall an anchor, and rode there (God be praiſed) in ſafety: but our other ſhips, riding without, were ſo oppreſſed with the extremitie of the ſtorme, that they were forced to run off to ſea for their owne ſafegard, being in good hope onely of the good ſucceſſe of that ſhip, which was gone in to relieue our generall; before this ſtorme aroſe,

arofe, our Caunter, formerly loft, was come in the fame day **1578.**
vnto vs into the roade, but was put to fea againe, the fame euening, with the reft of the fleete.

The next day May 14. the weather being faire, and the *May* 14.
windes moderate, but the fleet out of fight, our generall determined to goe afhore, to this end, that he might, by making of
fires, giue fignes to the difperfed fhips, to come together againe
into that roade: whereby at laft, they were all affembled, excepting the *Swanne*, loft long time before, and excepting our
Portugall prife, called the *Mary*; which waighing in this laft
ftorme, the night before, had now loft company, and was not
found againe in a long time after.

In this place (the people being remoued vp into tne country,
belike for feare of our comming) we found neere vnto the rocks,
in houfes made for that purpofe, as alfo in diuers other places,
great ftore of Oftriches at leaft to the number of 50. with much
other foule; fome dried and fome in drying for their prouifion,
as it feemed, to carrie with them to the place of their dwel-
lings. The Oftriches thighs were in bignes equall to reafonable
legs of mutton, They cannot flie at all; but they runne fo fwiftly,
and take fo long ftrides, that it is not poffible for a man in running by any meanes to take them, neither yet to come fo nigh
them, as to haue any fhot at them either with bow or peece:
Whereof our men had often proofe on other parts of that coaft
for all the countrey is full of them; We found there the tooles
or inftruments which the people vfe in taking them.

Among other meanes they vfe in betraying thefe Oftriches,
they haue a great and large plume of feathers, orderly compact together vpon the end of a ftaffe; in the forepart bearing the
likeneffe of the head, necke, and bulke of an Oftrich; and in the
hinder part, fpreading it felfe out very large, fufficient (being hol-
den before him) to hide the moft part of the body of a man:
With this it feemeth they ftaulke, driuing them into fome ftraite
or necke of land clofe to the fea fide; where fpreading long and
ftrong nets, with their dogs which they haue in readineffe at all
times,

times, they ouerthrow them, and make a common quarry. The countrey is very pleasant, and seemeth to be a fruitfull soyle.

Being afterwards driuen to fall with this place againe, we had great acquaintance and familiarity with the people, who reioyced greatly in our comming, and in our friendship, in that wee had done them no harme. But becaufe this place was no fit or conuenient harbor for vs, to do our neceffary bufines ; neither yet to make prouifion, of such things as we wanted, as water, *May 15.* wood, and such like, we departed thence the 15. of May.

At our departure hence, we held our courfe South and by Weft, and made about 9. leagues in 24. houres ; bearing very little fayle, that our fleet might the eafier gett vp with vs, which by reafon of the contrary windes, were caft a fterne of vs.

In 47. deg. 30. min. we found a bay, which was faire, fafe, and beneficiall to vs , very neceffary for our vfe ; into which *May 17.* we haled, and anchored May 17. and the next day May 18. we *May 18.* came further into the fame bay, where we caft anchor, and made our abode full fifteene dayes.

The very firft day of our arriuall here, our generall hauing fet things in fome order, for the difpatch of our neceffary bufines, being moft carefull for his two fhips which were wanting, fent forth to the fouthward, Captaine Winter in the Elizabeth viceadmiral; himfelf in the admiral, going forth northward, into the fea, to fee, if happily they might meete with either of them : at which time, by the good prouidence of God, hee himfelfe met with the Swanne, formerly loft at our departure from the riuer of Plate, and brought her into the fame harbor, the fame day : where being afterward vnloaden, and difcharged of her fraight, fhee was caft off, and her iron worke, and other neceffaries being faued, for the better prouifion of the reft ; of the remainder was made fire-wood, and other implements which we wanted. But all this while, of the other fhip which wee loft fo lately, in our extremitie, we could haue no newes.

While we were thus employed, after certaine dayes of our ftay in this place, being on fhoare, in an Iland, nigh vnto the
maine,

maine, where at lowe water was free paſſage on foot, from the one to the other; the people of the country did ſhew themſelues vnto vs, with leaping, dancing, and holding vp their hands, and making outcries after their manner : but being then high water, we could not go ouer to them on foot. Wherefore the Generall cauſed immediatly a boat to bee in readineſſe, and ſent vnto them ſuch things as he thought would delight them; as kniues, bells, bugles, and whereupon they beeing aſſembled together vpon a hill, halfe an Engliſh mile from the waters ſide, ſent downe two of their company, running one after the other with a great grace, trauerſing their ground as it ſeemed after the manner of their warres, by degrees deſcending towards the waters ſide very ſwiftly. Notwithſtanding drawing nigh vnto it, they made a ſtay, refuſing to come neere our men : which our men perceiuing, ſent ſuch things as they had tyed with a ſtring vpon a rod, and ſtucke the ſame vp a reaſonable diſtance from them, where they might ſee it. And aſſoone as our men were departed from the place, they came and tooke thoſe things, leauing inſtead of them, as in recompence, ſuch feathers as they vſe to weare about their heads, with a bone made in manner of a toothpick, carued round about the top, and in length about ſix inches, being very ſmoothly burniſhed. Whereupon our Generall, with diuers of his gentlemen and companie, at low water went ouer to them to the maine.

Againſt his comming they remained ſtill vpon the hill, and ſet themſelues in a ranke, one by one; appointing one of their company to runne before them from the one end of the ranke to the other, and ſo backe againe, continually Eaſt and Weſt, with holding vp his hands ouer his head, and yeelding forward his body in his running toward the riſing and ſetting of the Sunne: and at euery ſecond or third turne at the moſt, erected his body, againſt the midſt of the ranke of the people, lifting himſelfe vaulting-wiſe from the ground towards the Moone, being then ouer our heads: ſignifying thereby, as we conceiued, that they called the Sunne and Moone (whom they ſerue for gods)

gods)to witneſſe,that they meant nothing towards vs but peace. But when they perceiued that we aſcended the hill apace, and drew nigh vnto them, they ſeemed very fearefull of our comming.

Wherefore our Generall not willing, to giue them any way any occaſion to miſlike,or be diſcomfited, retyred his company; wherby they were ſo allured, and did ſo therein confirme themſelues of vs,that we were no enemies,neither meant them harm, that without al feare diuers came down with great ſpeed after vs, preſently entring into traffique with our men. Notwithſtanding they would receiue nothing at our hands but the ſame muſt be firſt caſt vpon the ground, vſing this word, *Zuſſus*, for exchange *Tóytt* to caſt vpon the ground. And if they miſliked any thing, they cryed *Coróh, Coróh,* ſpeaking the ſame with ratling in the throat. The wares we receiued from them were arrowes of reeds, feathers, and ſuch bones as are afore deſcribed.

This people go naked, except a skin of furre which they caſt about their ſhoulders, when they ſit or lye in the cold : but hauing any thing to do,as going or any other labour, they vſe it as a girdle about their loynes. They weare their haire very long,but leſt it might trouble them in their trauell, they knit it vp with a roll of Oſtrich feathers, vſing the ſame rolls and haire together for a quiuer for their arrowes, and for a ſtore houſe, in which they carry the moſt things which they carry about them. Some of them within theſe rolls ſticke on either ſide of their heads (for a ſigne of honour in their perſons)a large and plaine feather ſhewing like hornes afarre off : So that ſuch a head vpon a naked body (if diuels do appeare with hornes) might very nigh reſemble diuels.

Their whole brauery and ſetting out themſelues ſtandeth in painting their bodies with diuers colours , and ſuch workes as they can deuiſe. Some waſh their faces with ſulphure, or ſome ſuch like ſubſtance: ſome paint their whole bodies black,leauing onely their neckes behind and before white, much like our damoſels that weare their ſquares , their neckes and breaſts naked.

Some

Some paint one fhoulder blacke, another white; and their fides and legs interchangeably, with the fame colours, one ftill contrary to the other. The black part hath fet vpon it white moones, and the white part blacke Suns, being the marks and characters of their gods, as is before noted.

They haue fome commodity by painting of their bodies, for the which caufe they vfe it fo generally : and that I gather to be the defence it yeeldeth againft the piercing and nipping cold. For the colours being clofe layd on vpon their skinne, or rather in their flefh, as by continuall renewing of thefe iuyces which are layed on, foakt into the inner part thereof, doth fill vp the pores fo clofe that no aire or cold can enter, or make them once to fhrinke.

They haue cleane, comely, and ftrong bodies : they are fwift of foot, and feeme very actiue. Neither is any thing more lamentable (in my iudgement) then that fo goodly a people, and fo liuely creatures of God, fhould bee ignorant of the true and liuing God. And fo much the more is this to be lamented, by how much they are more tractable, and eafie to be brought to the fheepfold of Chrift : hauing in truth a land fufficient to recompence any Chriftian Prince in the world, for the whole trauell and labour, coft and charges beftowed in that behalfe : with a wonderfull enlarging of a kingdome, befides the glory of God by encreafing of the Church of Chrift.

Its wonderfull to heare, being neuer knowne to Chriftians before this time, how familiar they became in fhort fpace with vs; thinking themfelues to be ioyned with fuch a people, as they ought rather to ferue, then offer any wrong or iniurie vnto. Prefuming that they might be bold with our Generall as with a Father, and with vs as with brethren and their neereft friends; neither feemed their loue leffe towards vs. One of the chiefeft among them hauing on a time receiued a cap of our Generals head, which he did daily weare, remouing himfelfe but a little from vs, with an arrow pierced his legge deepely, caufing the bloud to ftreame out vpon the ground: fignifying thereby, how

vnfainedly

vnfainedly he loued him, and giuing therin a couenant of peace: The number of men which here did frequent our companie, were about fiftie perfons. Within, in the Southermoft part of this bay, there is a riuer of frefh water, with a great many profitable ilands; of which, fome haue alwaies fuch ftore of Seales or fea-wolues as were able to maintaine a huge army of men. Other Ilands being many and great, are fo replenifhed with birds and foule, as if there were no other victuals, a wonderfull multitude of people might be nourifhed by the increafe of them for many pofterities. Of thefe we killed fome with fhot, and fome with ftaues, and tooke fome with our hands, from mens heads and fhoulders vpon which they lighted. We could not perceiue that the people of the countrey had any fort of boate or canowe, to come to thefe Ilands. Their owne prouifion which they eate, for ought we could perceiue, was commonly raw. For we fhould fometimes find the remnants of Seales all bloudy which they had gnawne with their teeth like dogs: They go all of them armed, with a fhort bow of about an ell in length in their hands, with arrowes of reeds, and headed with a flint ftone, very cunningly cut and faftned.

  This bay by reafon of the plenty of *Seales* therein found (infomuch that we killed two hundred in the fpace of one houre) we called *Seale bay*. And hauing now made fufficient prouifion of victuals and other neceffaries, as alfo happily finifhed all our bufineffes, *Iune 3.* we fet faile from thence; And coafting along towards the pole Antartick *Iune 12.* we fell with a little bay, in which we anchored for the fpace of two dayes fpent in the difcharging of our Caunter, the Chriftopher, which wee here layed vp.

  The 14. day we waighed againe, and kept on our courfe Southward till the 17. and then caft anchor in another bay in 50. deg. 20. min. lacking but little more then one degree, of the mouth of the Straights, through which lay, our fo much defired paffage into the South fea.

  Here our generall on good aduife determined to alter his courfe,

courfe; and turne his fterne to the Northward againe, if happily God would grant we might find our fhip and friends whom we loft in the great ftorme, as is before faid. Forafmuch as (if we fhould enter the Straight without them in our company) it muft needs go hard with them; and we alfo in the meane time as well by their abfence, as by the vncertaintie of their ftate, muft needs receiue no fmall difcomfort.

And therefore Iune 18. in the morning putting to fea againe, with hartie and often prayers wee ioyned watchfull induftry to ferue Gods good prouidence: and held on our purpofe to runne backe toward the line into the fame height, in which they were firft diffeuered from vs.　　*Iune 18.*

The 19. day of Iune toward night, hauing fayled within a few leagues of port Saint *Iulian*, we had our fhip in fight: for which we gaue God thankes with moft ioyfull minds. And forafmuch as the fhip was farre out of order, and very leake, by reafon of extremity of weather which fhe had endured, afwell before her loofing company as in her abfence: our Generall thought good to beare into Port Saint *Iulian* with his fleet, becaufe it was fo nigh at hand, and fo conuenient a place: intending there to refrefh his wearied men, and cherifh them which had in their abfence tafted fuch bitterneffe of difcomfort, befides the want of many things which they fuftained.　　*Iune 19.*

Thus the next day the 20. of Iune we entred Port Saint *Iulian*: which ftandeth in 49. deg. 30. min. and hath on the South fide of the harbour picked rockes like towers, and within the harbour many Ilands, which you may ride hard aboard off, but in going in you muft borrow of the North fhoare.　　*Iune 20.*

Being now come to anchor, and all things fitted and made fafe aboard, our Generall with certaine of his companie, (viz. *Thomas Drake* his brother, *Iohn Thomas*, *Robert Winter*, *Oliuer* the Mafter gunner, *Iohn Brewer*, and *Thomas Hood*) Iune 22. rowed further in with a boate to find out fome conuenient place which might yeeld vs frefh water, during the time of our abode there, and furnifh vs with fupply for prouifion, to take to　　*Iune 22.*

ſea with vs at our departure. Which worke as it was of great neceſſitie, and therefore carefully to be performed; ſo did not he thinke himſelfe diſcharged of his duty, if he himſelfe beſtowed not the firſt trauell therein, as his vſe was at all times in all other things, belonging to the relieuing of our wants, and the maintenance of our good eſtate, by the ſupply of what was needfull. Preſently vpon his landing he was viſited by two of the inhabitants of the place, whom *Magellane* named *Patagons*, or rather *Pentagours* fron their huge ſtature, and ſtrength proportionable: Theſe as they ſeemed greatly to reioyce at his arriuall, ſo did they ſhew themſelues very familiar, receiuing at our Generals hands whatſoeuer he gaue them, and taking great pleaſure in ſeeing Maſter *Oliuer* the maſter gunner of the Admirall, to ſhoot an Engliſh arrow: trying with him to ſhoot at length, but came nothing neere him.

Not long after, came one more of the ſame laſte, but of a ſowerer ſorte, for he, miſliking of the familiarity which his fellowes had vſed, ſeemed very angry with them, and ſtroue earneſtly to withdrawe them, and to turne them to become our enemies; Which our generall with his men not ſuſpecting in thē, vſed them as before : and one Mr. Robert Winter, thinking of pleaſure to ſhoote an arrow at length, as Mr. Oliuer had done before, that he which came laſt alſo might haue a ſight thereof, the ſtring of his bow brake; which, as before it was a terror vnto them, ſo now broken, it gaue them great incouragement, and boldnes, and as they thought, great aduantage in their treacherous intent and purpoſe; not imagining that our calliuers, ſwords, and targets, were any munition or weapon of warre.

In which perſwaſion (as the generall with his companie were, quietly without any ſuſpition of euill, going downe towards his boate) they ſodainely being prepared, and gotten by ſtealth behinde them, ſhot their arrowes; and cheifely at him which had the bowe, not ſuffering him to ſtring the ſame againe, which he was about to haue done, as well as hee could: but being wounded in the ſhoulder at the firſt ſhot, and turning about,

abour, was fped with an arrow, which peirced his lunges, yet he
fell not. But the Mr. gunner being ready to fhoote of his calli-
uer, which tooke not fire in leuelling thereof, was prefently
flaine outright. In this extremitie, if our generall had not beene
both expert in fuch affaires, able to judge, and giue prefent direction in the danger thereof, and had not valiantly thruft himfelfe into the dance, againft thefe monfters, there had no one of
our men, that there were landed, efcaped with life. He therefore, giuing order that no man fhould keepe any certaine
ground, but fhift from place to place, encroaching ftill vpon the
enemie, vfing their targets, and other weapons for the defence
of their bodies, and that they fhould breake fo many arrowes, as
by any meanes they could come by, being fhot at them; wherein he himfelfe was very diligent, and carefull alfo in calling on
them, knowing that their arrowes being once fpent, they fhould
haue thefe enemies at their deuotion and pleafure, to kill or
faue, and this order being accordingly taken, himfelfe I fay with
a good courage and truft in the true and liuing God, taking and
fhooting off, the fame peece, which the gunner could not make
to take fire, difpatched the firft beginner of the quarrell, the fame
man which flewe our Mr. gunner. For the peece being charged
with a bullet, and haile fhot, and well aimed, tare out his bellie
and gutts, with great torment, as it feemed by his cry, which
was fo hideous and horrible a roare, as if ten bulls had ioyned
together in roaring, wherewith the courage of his partners was
fo abated, and their hearts appalled, that notwithftanding, diuerfe of their fellowes and countriemen appeared out of the
woods, on each fide: yet they were glad, by flying away, to
faue themfelues, quietly fuffering our men either to depart or
ftay. Our generall chofe rather to depart, then to take further
reuenge of them, which now he might, by reafon of his wounded man, whom for many good parts he loued dearely; and
therefore would rather haue faued him, then flaine an hundred
enemies, but being paft recouery, he died the 2. day, after his
being brought aboard againe.

That

That night our Mr. gunners body being left aſhoare, for the ſpeedier bringing of the other aboard, our generall himſelfe the next day, with his boate well appointed, returned to the ſhoare, to fetch it likewiſe: which they found lying where it was left, but ſtript of his vppermoſt garment, and hauing an engliſh arrow ſtrucke in his right eye.

Both of theſe dead bodies were layd together in one graue, with ſuch reuerence, as was fit for the earthen tabernacles of immortall ſoules; and with ſuch commendable ceremonies, as belong vnto ſouldiers of worth, in time of warre, which they moſt truly and rightfully deſerued.

Magellane was not altogether deceiued, in naming them Giants; for they generally differ from the common ſort of men, both in ſtature, bignes, and ſtrength of body, as alſo in the hideouſneſſe of their voice: but yet they are nothing ſo monſtrous, or giantlike as they were reported; there being ſome Engliſh men, as tall, as the higheſt of any that we could ſee, but peraduenture, the Spaniards did not thinke, that euer any Engliſh man would come thither, to reproue them; and therevpon might preſume the more boldly to lie: the name *Pentagones, Fiue cubits* viz. 7. foote and halfe, deſcribing the full height (if not ſome what more) of the higheſt of them.

But this is certaine, that the Spaniſh cruelties there vſed, haue made them more monſtrous, in minde and manners, then they are in body; and more inhoſpitable, to deale with any ſtrangers, that ſhall come hereafter. For the loſſe of their friends (the remembrance wherof is aſſigned and conueighed ouer from one generation to another, among their poſteritie) breedeth an old grudge, which will not eaſily be forgotten, with ſo quarrellſome and reuengefull a people. Notwithſtanding the terrour which they had conceiued of vs, did henceforward ſo quench their heate, and take downe their edge, that they both forgate reuenge, and ſeeming by their countenance, to repent them of the wrong they had offered vs, that meant them no harme, ſuffered vs to doe what we would, the whole ſpace of

two

two monethes after this, without any interruption or molesta-
tion by them, and it may perhaps be a meanes, to breede
a peace in that people, towards all that may hereafter this,
come that way.

To this euill, thus receiued at the hands of infidells, there was
adioyned, and grew another mischiefe, wrought and contriued
closely amongst our selues, as great, yea farre greater, and of farre
more greiuous consequence then the former: but that it was,
by Gods prouidence, detected and preuented in time, which
else had extended it selfe, not onely to the violent shedding of
innocent blood, by murthering our generall and such others as
were most firme and faithfull to him: but also to the finall ouerthrow of the whole action intended, and to diuers other most
dangerous effects.

These plotts had beene layd before the voyage beganne in
England: the very modell of them was shewed, and declared to
our generall in his garden at Plimmouth, before his setting sayle,
which yet he either would not credit, as true or likely, of a person whom he loued so deerely, and was perswaded of to loue
him likewise vnfainedly, or thought by loue and benefits, to remoue and remedy it, if there were any euill purposes conceiued
against him.

And therfore, he did not onely continue (to this suspected &
accused person) al countenance, credit, and courtesies, which he
was wont to shew & giue him; but encreased them, vsing him in
a manner as another himselfe, and as his most inmost friend:
lodging him with himselfe; giuing him the second place, in all
companies, in his presence; leauing in his hand, the state as it
were of his owne person, in his absence; imparting vnto him
all his counsells; allowing him free liberty in all things, that
were reasonable; and bearing often, at his hands great infirmi-
ties; yea despising, that any priuate iniury, should breake so
firme a friendship, as he meant towards him. And therefore, was
he often times not a little offended, euen with those, who (vpon
conscience of their duty, and knowledge that otherwise they

E   should

should indeed offend)diſcloſed from time to time vnto him, how the fire increaſed, that theatned his owne, together with the deſtruction of the whole action.

But at length, perceiuing that his lenity and fauours did little good; in that the heat of ambition was not yet allayed, nor could be quenched, as it ſeemed, but by blood; and that the manifold practiſes grew dayly more and more, euen to extremities; he thought it high time, to call theſe practiſes into queſtion, before it were too late, to call any queſtion of them into hearing. And therefore ſetting good watch ouer him, and aſſembling all his Captaines, and gentlemen of his comapany together; he propounded to them, the good parts which were in the gentleman, the great good will, and inward affection, more then brotherly, which he had euer, ſince his firſt acquaintance borne him, not omitting the reſpect, which was had of him, among no meane perſonages in England; and afterwards deliuered the letters, which were written to him, with the particulars from time to time, which had beene obſerued, not ſo much by himſelfe, as by his good friends; not onely at ſea, but euen at Plimmouth; not bare words but writings; not writings alone, but actions, tending to the ouerthrowe of the ſeruice in hand, and making away of his perſon.

Proofes were required and alleaged, ſo many, and ſo euident, that the gentleman himſelfe, ſtricken with remorſe of his inconſiderate and vnkinde dealing, acknowledged himſelfe to haue deſerued death, yea many deathes; for that he conſpired, not onely the ouerthrow of the action, but of the principall actor alſo, who was not a ſtranger or il-willer, but a deare and true friend vnto him: and therefore in a great aſſembly openly beſought them, in whoſe hands iuſtice reſted, to take ſome order for him; that he might not be compelled, to enforce his owne hands, againſt his owne bowells, or otherwiſe to become his owne executioner.

The admiration and aſtoniſhment hereat, in all the hearers euen thoſe which were his neereſt friends, and moſt affected him
was

was great, yea in thofe, which for many benefits receiued from him, had good caufe to loue him : but yet the generall was moft of all diftracted ; and therefore withdrewe himfelfe, as not able to conceale his tender affection, requiring them, that had heard the whole matter, to giue their iudgements, as they would another day anfwer it vnto their prince, and vnto almightie God, judge of all the earth. Therefore they all, aboue 40. in number, the chiefeft of place and judgement in the whole fleet, after they had difcuffed diuerfly of the cafe, and alleaged what-foeuer came in their mindes, or could be there produced by any of his other friends, with their owne hands, vnder feale, adiudged that : *He had deferued death* : *And that it ftoode, by no meanes with their fafety, to let him liue* : *And therefore, they remitted the manner thereof, with the reft of the circumftances to the generall.*

This judgement, and as it were affife, was held a land, in one of the Ilands of that port ; which afterwards, in memory hereof was called, the Iland of *True iuftice and iudgement.*

Now after this verdict was thus returned vnto our generall (vnto whom, for his company, her maieftie before his depar-ture, had committed her fword, to vfe for his fafety, with this word : *We doe account that he which ftriketh at thee Drake ftriketh at vs*)he called for the guilty party, and caufed to be read vnto him, the feuerall verdicts which were written, and pronounced of him, which being acknowledged for the moft part (for none had giuen heauier fentence againft him, then he had giuen a-gainft himfelfe) our generall propofed vnto him this choice : *Whether he would take, to be executed in this Iland ? or to be fett a-land on the maine ? or returne into England, there to anfwer his deed before the Lords of her maiefties Councell ?*

He moft humbly thanked the generall for his clemencie, ex-tended towards him in fuch ample fort : and crauing fome ref-pit, to confult thereon, and fo make his choice aduifedly : the next day he returned this anfwer, that : *Albeit he had yeelded in his heart, to entertaine fo great a finne ; as whereof now he was iuft-ly condemned : yet he had a care, and that excelling all other cares,*

E 2   *to*

to die a christian man, that whatsoeuer did become of his clay body, he might yet remaine assured of an eternall inheritance, in a farre better life. This he feared, if he should be set a land among Infidels, how he should be able to maintaine this assurance, feeling in his owne frailtie, how mighty the contagion is of lewde custome. And therefore he besought the generall most earnestly, that *he would yet haue a care, and regard of his soule; and neuer ieopard it amongst heathen and sauage Infidells. If he should returne into England, he must first haue a ship, and men to conduct it, with sufficient victuals: two of which though they were had, yet for the third, he thought no man would accompanie him, in so bad a message to so vile an issue, from so honorable a seruice. But if that there were, which could induce their mindes, to returne with him; yet the very shame of the returne, would be as death, or grieuouser if it were possible: because he should be so long a dying, and die so often. Therefore he professed, that with all his heart, he did embrace the first branch of the generals proffer; desiring onely this fauour, that they might receiue the holy communion, once againe together before his death; and that he might not die, other then a gentlemans death.*

Though sundry reasons were vsed by many, to perswade him to take either of the other wayes: yet when he remained resolute in his former determination, both parts of his last request were granted: and the next conuenient day, a communion was celebrated, by *Mr. Francis Fletcher,* preacher and pastor of the fleet at that time. The generall himselfe communicated in this Sacred ordinance, with this condemned penitent gentleman; who shewed great tokens of a contrite and repentant heart, as who was more deepely displeased with his owne act, then any man else. And after this holy repast, they dined also at the same table together, as cheerefully in sobriety, as euer in their liues they had done aforetime: each cheering vp the other, and taking their leaue, by drinking each to other, as if some journey onely had beene in hand.

After dinner, all things being brought in a readines, by him that supplied the roome of the prouost Marshall; without any

dallying

dallying, or delaying the time, he came forth, and kneeled downe, preparing at once, his necke for the axe, and his spirit for heauen: which hauing done, without long ceremony, as who had before digested this whole tragedy, he desired all the rest to pray for him, and willed the executioner to doe his office, not to feare nor spare.

Thus hauing by the worthie manner of his death (being much more honorable by it, then blameable for any other of his actions) fully blotted out, what euer staine, his fault might seeme to bring vpon him; he left vnto our fleete, a lamentable example of a goodly gentleman, who in seeking aduancement vnfit for him, cast away himselfe: and vnto posteritie a monument, of I know not what, fatall calamitie, incident to that Port, and such like actions, which might happilie afford a new paire of paralells, to be added to Plutarchs: in that the same place, neere about the same time of the yeare, witnessed the execution of 2. gentlemen, suffring both for the like cause, employed both in like seruice, entertained both in great place, endued both with excellent qualities, the one 58. yeare after the other.

For on the maine, our men found a gibbet, fallen downe, made of a spruce mast, with mens bones vnderneath it, which they coniectured to be the same gibbet, which Magellane commanded to be erected, in the yeare 1520. for the execution, of *Iohn Carthagene* the Bishop of Burgos cosen, who by the kings order, was ioyned with Magellane in commission, and made his vice-admirall.

In the Iland, as we digged to burie this gentleman, we found a great grinding stone, broken in two parts, which wee tooke and set fast in the ground, the one part at the head, the other at the feet, building vp the middle space, with other stones and turfes of earth, and engraued in the stones, the names of the parties buried there, with the time of their departure, and a memoriall of our generalls name in Latine, that it might the better be vnderstood, of all that should come after vs.

These things thus ended, and set in order, our generall discharging

charging the *Mary* viz. our Portugall prife, becaufe fhee was leake and troublefome, defaced her; and then left her ribs and keele vpon the Iland : where for two moneths together we had pitched our tents. And fo hauing wooded, watered, trimmed our fhips, difpatched all our other bufineffes, and brought our fleet into the fmalleft number, euen 3. onely, befides our pinnaces, that we might the eafier keepe our felues together, be the better furnifhed with neceffaries, and be the ftronger mand, againft whatfoeuer need fhould be, Auguft 17. we departed out of this port, and being now in great hope, of a happie iffue to our enterprife, which almighty god hitherto had fo bleft and profpered, we fet our courfe for the Straights. Southweft.

Auguft 20. we fel with the cape ; neere which lies the entrance into the ftraight, called by the Spaniards *Capo virgin Maria,* appearing 4. leagues before you come to it with high and fteepe gray cliffes, full of blacke ftarres, againft which the fea beating, fheweth as it were the fpoutings of Whales, hauing the higheft of the cape, like cape vincent in Portugall: At this cape, our generall caufed his fleet, in homage to our foueraigne lady the Queenes maiefty, to ftrike their top-failes vpon the bunt, as a token of his willing and glad minde, to fhewe his dutifull obedience to her highnes, whom he acknowledged to haue full intereft and right, in that new difcouery ; and withall, in remembrance of his honorable friend and fauorer, *Sir Chriftopher Hatton,* he changed the name of the fhippe, which himfelfe went in, from the *Pellican* to be called *the golden Hinde.* Which ceremonies being ended, together with a fermon, teaching true obedience, with prayers and giuing of thankes for her maiefty, and moft honorable counfell, with the whole body of the common weale, and church of God, we continued our courfe on into the faid frete, where paffing with land in fight on both fides, we fhortly fell with fo narrow a ftraite, as carrying with it much winde, often turnings, and many dangers, requireth an expert judgement, in him that fhall paffe the fame, it lieth Weft North Weft & Eaft South Eaft: but hauing left this ftraite a fterne, we

seemed

seemed to be come out of a riuer of two leagues broade, into a large and maine sea; hauing the night following, an Iland in sight, which (being in height nothing inferior to the Iland *Fogo*, before spoken of) burneth (like it also) aloft in the aire, in a wonderfull sort, without intermiffion.

It hath formerly beene receiued as an vndoubted truth, that the seas, following the courfe of the firft mouer, from Eaft to Weft, haue a continuall current through this ftraite, but our experience found the contrary: the ebbings and flowings here, being as orderly (in which the water rifes and falls more then 5. fathomes, vpright) as on other coafts.

The 24. of Auguft being Bartholomew day, we fell with 3. Ilands, bearing triangle-wife one from another, one of them was very faire and large, and of a fruitfull foile, vpon which being next vnto vs, and the weather very calme, our generall with his gentlemen, and certaine of his mariners, then landed, taking poffeffion thereof in her Maiefties name, and to her vfe, and called the fame *Elizabeth* Iland.

The other two, though they were not fo large, nor fo faire to the eye, yet were they to vs exceeding vfefull; for in them wee found great ftore of ftrange birds, which could not flie at all, nor yet runne fo faft, as that they could efcape vs with their liues: in body they are leffe then a goofe, and bigger then a mallard, fhort and thicke fet together, hauing no feathers, but infteed thereof, a certaine hard and matted downe; their beakes are not much vnlike the bills of crowes, they lodge and breed vpon the land, where making earthes, as the conies doe, in the ground, they lay their egges, and bring vp their young; their feeding and prouifion to liue on, is in the fea, where they fwimm in fuch fort, as nature may feeme to haue granted them no fmall prerogatiue in fwiftneffe, both to prey vpon others, and themfelues to efcape from any others that feeke to ceafe vpon them, and fuch was the infinite refort of thefe birds to thefe Ilands, that in the fpace of 1. day, we killed no leffe then 3000. & if the increafe be according to the number, it is not to be thought, that the world hath

hath brought forth, a greater bleſſing in one kinde of creature in ſo ſmall a circuit, ſo neceſſarily and plentifully ſeruing the vſe of man, they are a very good and wholeſome victuall : our generall named theſe Ilands, the one *Bartholomew*, according to the day ; the other Saint *Georges*, in honour of England, according to the ancient cuſtome there obſerued.

In the Iland of Saint *George*, we found the body of a man, ſo long dead before, that his bones would not hold together, being moued out of the place whereon they lay.

From theſe Ilands, to the entrance into the South ſea, the frete is very crooked; hauing many turnings, and as it were ſhuttings vp, as if there were no paſſage at all, by meanes whereof, we were often troubled with contrary windes, ſo that ſome of our ſhips, recouering a cape of land, entring another reach, the reſt were forced to alter their courſe, and come to anchor where they might. It is true which Magellane reporteth of this paſſage : namely that there be many faire harbours, and ſtore of freſh water ; but ſome ſhips, had need to be fraughted with nothing elſe, beſides anchors and cables, to finde ground, in moſt of them, to come to anchor ; which when any extreame guſts, or contrary windes doe come(whereunto the place is altogether, ſubiect)is a great hindrance to the paſſage, and carrieth with it no ſmall danger.

The land on both ſides is very high and mountainous, hauing on the North and Weſt ſide the continent of America, and on the South and Eaſt part, nothing but Ilands : among which, lye innumerable fretes or paſſages into the South ſea. The mountaines ariſe with ſuch tops, and ſpires into the aire, & of ſo rare a height, as they may well be accounted amongſt the wonders of the world ; enuironed as it were, with many regions of congealed clouds, and frozen meteors, wherby they are continually fed and increaſed, both in height and bignes, from time to time, retaining that which they haue once receiued, being little againe diminiſhed by the heate of the ſun, as being ſo farre from reflexion, and ſo nigh the cold and frozen region.

But

But notwithſtanding all this, yet are the lowe and plaine groundes verie fruitful, the graſſe greene and naturall; the hearbs that are of very ſtrange ſorts, good and many; the trees for the moſt part of them alwaies greene; the ayre of the temperature of our countrey; the water moſt pleaſant; and the ſoile agreeing to any graine which we haue growing in our countrie: a place no doubt, that lacketh nothing, but a people to vſe the ſame to the Creators glory, and the encreaſing of the Church: the people inhabiting theſe parts, made fires as we paſſed by in diuers places.

Drawing nigh the entrance of the South ſea, wee had ſuch a ſhutting vp to the Northwards, and ſuch large and open fretes toward the South, that it was doubtfull which way wee ſhould paſſe, without further diſcouerie: for which cauſe, our generall hauing brought his fleete to anchor vnder an Iland; himſelfe, with certaine of his gentlemen, rowed in a boate to deſcrie the paſſage; who hauing diſcouered a ſufficient way towards the North, in their returne to their ſhips, met a cannowe vnder the ſame Iland, where wee rode then at anchor, hauing in her diuers perſons.

This cannowe or boate was made of the barke of diuers trees, hauing a prowe and a ſterne ſtanding vp, and ſemicircle-wiſe yeelding inward, of one forme and faſhion; the body whereof was a moſt dainty mould, bearing in it moſt comely proportion, and excellent workmanſhip; in ſo much as to our generall and vs, it ſeemed neuer to haue beene done, without the cunning and expert iudgement of art; and that not for the vſe of ſo rude and barborous a people, but for the pleaſure of ſome great and noble perſonage, yea of ſome Prince: It had no other cloſing vp or caulking in the ſeames, but the ſtitchin with thongs, made of Seale-skins, or other ſuch beaſt, and yet ſo cloſe that it receiued very little or no water at all.

The people are of a meane ſtature, but well ſet and compact, in all their parts and limmes; they haue great pleaſure in painting their faces, as the others haue, of whom we haue ſpoken

F　　　　　　　　　　before:

before. Within the said Iland they had a house of meane building, of certaine poles, and couered with skinnes of beasts; hauing therein fire, water, and such meate, as commonly they can come by: as seales, muffels, and such like.

The vessels wherein they keepe their water, and their cups in which they drinke, are made of barkes of trees, as was their canow: and that with no lesse skill (for the bignesse of the thing) being of a very formall shape and good fashion. Their working tooles, which they vse in cutting these things and such other, are kniues made of most huge and monstrous mussell shels (the like whereof haue not beene seene or heard of lightly by any trauellers; the meate thereof beeing very sauourie and good in eating) which, after they haue broken off the thinne and brittle substance of the edge, they rub and grinde them vpon stones had for the purpose, till they haue tempered and set such an edge vpon them, that no wood is so hard but they will cut it at pleasure with the same: whereof we our selues had experience. Yea they cut therewith bones of a maruellous hardnesse; making of them fisgies to kill fish, wherein they haue a most pleasant exercise with great dexteritie.

The sixth of September we had left asterne vs all these troublesome Ilands, and were entred into the South sea, or *Mare del zur*: at the cape whereof, our Generall had determined with his whole company to haue gone ashore, and there after a Sermon to haue left a monument of her Maiestie ingrauen in mettall, for a perpetuall remembrance; which he had in a readinesse for that end prepared: but neither was there any anchoring, neither did the wind suffer vs by any meanes to make a stay.

Onely this by all our mens obseruations was concluded; that the entrance, by which we came into this straite, was in 52. deg. the middest in 53. deg. 15. m. and the going out in 52. deg. 30. m. being 150. leagues in length: At the very entry, supposed also to be about 10. leagues in bredth. After we were entred ten leagues within it, it was found not past a league in breadth: farther within, in some places very large, in some very narrow, and

in

in the end found to be no straite at all, but all Ilands.

Now when our Generall perceiued that the nipping cold, vnder so cruell and frowning a Winter, had empaired the health of some of his men ; hee meant to haue made the more haste againe toward the line, and not to saile any farther towards the pole Antartick, lest being farther from the Sunne, and neerer the cold, we might happily be ouertaken with some greater danger of sicknesse. But God giuing men leaue to purpose, reserueth to himselfe the disposition of all things : making their intents of none effect, or changing their meanings oft times cleane into the contrary, as may best serue for his owne glory and their profit.

For September 7. the second day after our entrance into the South sea (called by some *Mare pacificum*, but prouing to vs rather to be *Mare furiosum*.) God by a contrary wind and intollerable tempest, seemed to set himselfe against vs : forcing vs not onely to alter our course and determination, but with great trouble, long time, many dangers, hard escapes, and finall separating of our fleet, to yeeld our selues vnto his will. Yea such was the extremitie of the tempest, that it appeared to vs as if he had pronounced a sentence, not to stay his hand, nor to withdraw his iudgement till he had buried our bodies and ships also, in the bottomlesse depth of the raging sea.

Sept. 7.

In the time of this incredible storme the 15. of September, the Moone was ecclipsed in Aries, and darkened about three points, for the space of two glasses : which being ended, might seeme to giue vs some hope of alteration and change of weather to the better. Notwithstanding, as the ecclipticall conflict could adde nothing to our miserable estate, no more did the ending thereof ease vs any thing at all ; nor take away any part of our troubles from vs: but our ecclipse continued still in its full force, so preuailing against vs, that for the space of full 52. dayes together, we were darkened more then the Moone by 20. parts, or more then we by any meanes could euer haue preserued, or recouered light of our selues againe, if the Sonne of God which

Sept. 15.

layed

layed this burthen vpon our backs, had not mercifully borne it vp with his owne shoulders, and vpheld vs in it by his owne power, beyond any possible strength or skill of man. Neither indeed did we at all escape, but with the feeling of great discomforts through the same.

For these violent and extraordinarie flawes (such as seldome haue beene seene) still continuing, or rather increasing, Septem-

Sept.30. ber 30. in the night, caused the sorrowfull separation of the *Marigold* from vs, in which was Captaine *Iohn Thomas*, with many others of our deare friends: who by no means that we could conceiue could helpe themselues, but by spooming along before the sea. With whom albeit wee could neuer meet againe, yet (our Generall hauing aforehand giuen order, that if any of our fleet did loose company, the place of resort to meet againe should be in 30. deg. or thereabouts, vpon the coast of Peru, toward the Equinoctiall) wee long time hoped (till experience shewed our hope was vaine) that there we should ioyfully meet with them: especially for that they were well prouided of victuals, and lackt no skilfull and sufficient men (besides their Captaine) to bring forwards the ship to the place appointed.

From the seuenth of September (in which the storme began)

Octob.7. till the seuenth of October we could not by any meanes recouer any land (hauing in the meane time beene driuen so farre South, as to the 57. deg. and somewhat better) on this day towards night, somewhat to the Northward of that cape of America (whereof mention is made before in the description of our departure from the straite into this sea) with a sorrie saile wee entred a harbour: where hoping to enioy some freedome and ease, till the storme was ended, we receiued within few houres after our comming to anchor, so deadly a stroake and hard entertainement, that our Admirall left not onely an anchor behind her, through the violence and furie of the flawe; but in departing thence, also lost the company and sight of our Vice-admirall, the *Elizabeth*: partly through the negligence of those that had the charge of her, partly through a kind of desire that some in

her

her had to be out of these troubles, and to be at home againe: which (as since is knowne) they thence forward by all meanes assayed and performed. For the very next day October 8. recouering the mouth of the straits againe (which wee were now so neere vnto) they returned backe the same way by which they came forward, and so coasting Brasill, they arriued in England Iune 2. the yeare following.

So that now our Admirall if she had retained her old name of Pellican, which she bare at our departure from our countrey, she might haue beene now indeed said to be as a Pellican alone in the wildernesse. For albeit our Generall sought the rest of his fleet with great care, yet could we not haue any sight or certaine newes of them by any meanes.

From this bay of parting of friends, we were forcibly driuen backe againe into 55. deg. towards the pole Antarticke. In which height we ranne in among the Ilands before mentioned, lying to the Southward of America, through which we passed from one sea to the other, as hath beene declared. Where comming to anchor, wee found the waters there to haue their indraught and free passage, and that through no small guts, or narrow channels, but indeed through as large frets or straights, as it hath at the supposed streights of Magellane through which we came.

Among these Ilands, making our abode with some quietnesse for a very little while, (viz. two dayes) and finding diuers good and wholesome herbs together with fresh water; our men which before were weake, and much empaired in their health, began to receiue good comfort: especially by the drinking of one herbe (not much vnlike that herbe which wee commonly call Penny-leafe) which purging with great facilitie affoorded great helpe and refreshing to our wearied and sickly bodies. But the winds returning to their old wont, and the seas raging after their former manner, yea euery thing as it were setting it selfe against our peace and desired rest, here was no stay permitted vs, neither any safety to be looked for.

1578.

Octob. 8.

For

For such was the present danger by forcing and continuall flawes, that we were rather to looke for present death then hope for any deliuery, if God almightie should not make the way for vs. The winds were such as if the bowels of the earth had set all at libertie; or as if all the clouds vnder heauen had beene called together, to lay their force vpon that one place: The seas, which by nature and of themselues are heauie, and of a weightie substance, were rowled vp from the depths, euen from the roots of the rockes, as if it had beene a scroll of parchment, which by the extremity of heate runneth together: and being aloft were carried in most strange manner and abundance, as feathers or drifts of snow, by the violence of the winds, to water the exceeding tops of high and loftie mountaines. Our anchors, as false friends in such a danger, gaue ouer their holdfast, and as if it had beene with horror of the thing, did shrinke downe to hide themselues in this miserable storme; committing the distressed ship and helpelesse men to the vncertaine and rowling seas, which tossed them, like a ball in a racket. In this case, to let fall more anchors, would auaile vs nothing; For being driuen from our first place of anchoring, so vnmeasurable was the depth, that 500. fathome would fetch no ground: So that the violent storme without intermission; the impossibility to come to anchor; the want of opportunitie to spread any sayle; the most mad seas; the lee shores; the dangerous rocks; the contrary and most intollerable winds; the impossible passage out; the desperate tarrying there; and ineuitable perils on euery side, did lay before vs so small likelihood to escape present destruction, that if the speciall prouidence of God himselfe had not supported vs, we could neuer haue endured that wofull state: as being inuironed with most terrible and most fearefull iudgements round about. For truly, it was more likely that the mountaines should haue beene rent in sunder, from the top to the bottome, and cast headlong into the sea, by these vnnaturall winds; then that we, by any helpe or cunning of man, should free the life of any one amongst vs.

Notwithstanding the same God of mercy which deliuered

Ionas

Ionas out of the VVhales belly, and heareth all those that call vpon him faithfully, in their diſtreſſe; looked downe from heauen, beheld our teares, and heard our humble petitions, ioyned with holy vowes. Euen God (whom not the winds and ſeas al one, but euen the diuels themſelues and powers of hell obey) did ſo wonderfully free vs, and make our way open before vs, as it were by his holy Angels ſtill guiding and conducting vs, that more then the affright and amaze of this eſtate, we receiued no part of damage in all the things that belonged vnto vs.

But eſcaping from theſe ſtraites and miſeries, as it were through the needles ey (that God might haue the greater glory in our deliuery) by the great and effectuall care and trauell of our Generall, the Lords inſtrument therein ; we could now no longer forbeare, but muſt needes finde ſome place of refuge, aſwell to prouide water, wood, and other neceſſaries, as to comfort our men, thus worne and tired out, by ſo many and ſo long intollerable toyles : the like whereof, its to be ſuppoſed, no traueller hath felt, neither hath there euer beene, ſuch a tempeſt (that any records make mention of) ſo violent, and of ſuch continuance, ſince *Noahs* flood, for as hath beene ſayd it laſted from September 7. to October 28, full 52. dayes.

Not many leagues therefore to the Southwards of our former anchoring, we ranne in againe among theſe Ilands ; where we had once more better likelihood to reſt in peace: and ſo much the rather, for that wee found the people of the countrie, trauelling for their liuing, from one Iland to another, in their canowes, both men, women, and young infants wrapt in skins, and hanging at their mothers backs ; with whom we had traffique, for ſuch things as they had, as chaines of certaine ſhells and ſuch other trifles ; here the Lord gaue vs three dayes to breath our ſelues, and to prouide ſuch things as we wanted, albeit the ſame was with continuall care, and troubles to auoid imminent dangers, which the troubled ſeas and bluſtering windes, did euery houre threaten vnto vs.

But when we ſeemed to haue ſtayed there too long, we were

more

more rigorously affaulted by the not formerly ended, but now more violently renewed ftorme; and driuen thence alfo with no fmall danger; leauing behind vs the greater part of our cable with the anchor; being chafed along by the winds, and buffeted inceffantly in each quarter by the feas(which our Generall interpreted, as though God had fent them of purpofe to the end which enfued) till at length wee fell with the vttermoft part of land towards the South pole,and had certainely difcouered how farre the fame doth reach Southward,from the coaft of America aforenamed.

The vttermoft cape or hedland of all thefe Ilands, ftands neere in 56. deg. without which there is no maine, nor Iland to be feene to the Southwards: but that the Atlanticke Ocean,and the South fea, meete in a moft large and free fcope.

It hath beene a dreame through many ages, that thefe Ilands haue beene a maine, and that it hath beene *terra incognita*; wherein many ftrange monfters liued. Indeed it might truly; before this time, be called *incognota*, for howfoeuer the mappes and generall defcriptions of *Cofmographers*, either vpon the deceiueable reports of other men, or the deceitfull imaginations of themfelues(fuppofing neuer herein to be corrected)haue fet it downe, yet it is true, that before this time, it was neuer difcouered, or certainely knowne by any traueller, that wee haue heard of.

And here as in a fit place, it fhall not be amiffe, to remoue that error in opinion, which hath beene held by many, of the impoffible returne, out of *Mar Del Zur*, into the Weft Ocean; by reafon of the fuppofed Eafterne current, and leuant windes: which(fay they)fpeedily carrie any thither, but fuffer no returne. They are herein likewife altogether deceiued : for neither did we meete with any fuch current,neither had we any fuch certaine windes, with any fuch fpeed to carry vs through; but at all times, in our paffage there, we found more opportunity to returne backe againe, into the Weft Ocean,then to goe forward into *Mar Del Zur*, by meanes either of current, or windes to
hinder

hinder vs, whereof we had experience more then we wifhed: being glad oftentimes, to alter our courfe, and to fall afterne againe, with francke winde (without any impediment of any fuch furmifed current) farther in one afternoone, then we could fetch vp, or recouer againe in a whole day, with a reafonable gale. And in that they alleage the narrownes of the frete, and want of fea-roome, to be the caufe of this violent current; they are herein no leffe deceiued, then they were in the other without reafon : for befides, that it cannot be fayd, that there is one onely paffage, but rather innumerable ; it is moft certaine, that a fea-board all thefe Ilands, there is one large and maine fea, wherein if any will not be fatisfied, nor belieue the report of our experience and ey-fight, hee fhould be aduifed to fufpend his iudgement, till he haue either tried it himfelfe, by his owne trauell, or fhall vnderftand, by other trauellers, more particulars to confirme his minde herein.

Now as wee were fallen to the vttermoft part of thefe Ilands Octob. 28.our troubles did make an end, the ftorme ceafed, and all our calamities (onely the abfence of our friends excepted) were remoued, as if God, all this while, by his fecret prouidence, had lead vs to make this difcouery; which being made, according to his will he ftayed his hand, as pleafed his maieftie therein, and refrefhed vs as his feruants. *Octob.* 28.

At thefe Southerly parts we found the night, in the latter end of October, to be but 2. houres long : the funne being yet aboue 7. degrees diftant from the Tropick : fo that it feemeth, being in the Tropick, to leaue very little, or no night at all in that place.

There be few of all thefe Ilands, but haue fome inhabitants, whofe manners, apparell, houfes, canowes and meanes of liuing, is like vnto thofe formerly fpoken of, a little before our departure out of the *Straight.* To all thefe Ilands, did our generall giue one name, to wit *Elizabethides.*

After two daies ftay, which wee made in and about thefe Ilands, the 30. of October we fet faile; fhaping our courfe right *Octob.*30.

Northweft, to coaft alongft the parts of *Peru*(for fo the generall mappes fet out the land to lie)both for that we might, with con-uenient fpeed, full with the height of 30. deg. being the place appointed, for the reft of our fleete to re-affemble ; as alfo, that no opportunity might be loft, in the meane time to finde them out, if it feemed good to God to direct them to vs.

In this courfe, we chanced(the next day)with two Ilands, being as it were ftore-houfes, of moft liberall prouifion of victu-alls for vs, of birds; yeelding not onely fufficient and plentifull ftore, for vs who were prefent, but enough, to haue ferued all the reft alfo, which were abfent.

Thence (hauing furnifhed our felues to our content)we con-tinued our courfe Nouember 1. ftill Northweft, as wee had formerly done, but in going on, we foone efpied, that we might eafily haue beene deceiued : and, therefore cafting about, and fteering vpon another point, wee found, that the generall mappes did erre from the truth, in fetting downe the coaft of *Pe-ru*, for 12. deg. at leaft to the Northward, of the fuppofed ftraite; no leffe then is the Northweft point of the compaffe, different from the Northeaft, perceiuing hereby, that no man; had euer by trauell, difcouered any part of thefe 12. deg. and therefore the fetters forth of fuch defcriptions, are not to be trufted; much leffe honored, in their falfe and fraudulent con-iectures; which they vfe, not in this alone, but in diuers other points of no fmall importance.

We found this part of *Peru*, all alongft to the height of *Lima*, which is 12. deg. South of the line, to be mountainous and ve-ry barren, without water or wood, for the moft part, except in certaine places, inhabited by the Spaniards, and few others, which are very fruitfull and commodious.

After we were once againe thus fallen with the land, we conti-nually coafted along, til we came to the height of 37. d. or there-about : and finding no conuenient place of abode, nor likeli-hood to heare any newes of our fhips, we ranne off againe with an Iland, which lay in fight, named of the Spaniards *Mucho*, by reafon reason of the greatnesse and large circuit thereof.

At this Iland comming to anchor, Nouemb.25.we found it to be a fruitfull place, and well stored with sundrie sorts of good things: as sheepe and other cattell, maize, which is a kinde of graine whereof they make bread, potatoes, with such other rootes: besides that, it is thought to be wonderfull rich in gold and to want no good thing for the vse of mans life. The inhabitants are such Indians, as by the cruell and most extreame dealing of the Spaniards, haue beene driuen to flie from the maine, here to releeue and fortifie themselues. With this people, our Generall thought it meet to haue traffique, for fresh victuals and water : and for that cause, the very same night of our arriuall there, himselfe with diuers of his company went ashoare, to whom the people with great courtesie came downe, bringing with them such fruits and other victuals as they had, and two very fat sheepe, which they gaue our Generall for a present. In recompence whereof, hee bestowed vpon them againe many good and necessarie things; signifying vnto them, that the end of his comming was for no other cause but by way of exchange, to traffique with them for such things as wee needed, and they could spare : and in particular, for such as they had alreadie brought downe vnto vs, besides fresh water, which wee desired of them. Herein they held themselues well contented, and seemed to be not a little ioyful of our comming: appointing where we should the next morning haue fresh water at pleasure, and withall signifying that then also they would bring vs downe such other things as we desired to serue our turnes.

The next day therefore very early in the morning (all things being made readie for traffique, as also vessels prepared to bring the water) our Generall taking great care for so necessarie prouision, repaired to the shoare againe ; and setting aland two of his men, sent them with their *Barricoes* to the watering place, assigned the night before. Who hauing peaceably past on one halfe of the way, were then with no small violence set vpon by those traiterous people, and suddenly slaine: And to the end that

our

our Generall with the rest of his company should not onely be stayed from rescuing them, but also might fall (if it were possible) into their hands in like manner, they had layed closely behind the rockes an ambushment of (as we guessed) about 500. men, armed and well appointed for such a mischiefe. Who suddenly attempting their purpose (the rocks being very dangerous for the boate, and the sea-gate exceeding great) by shooting their arrowes hurt and wounded euery one of our men, before they could free themselues, or come to the vse of there weapons to do any good. The General himself was shot in the face, vnder his right eye, and close by his nose, the arrow piercing a maruellous way in, vnder *basis cerebri*, with no small danger of his life; besides that, he was grieuously wounded in the head. The rest, being nine persons in the boate, were deadly wounded in diuers parts of their bodies, if God almost miraculously had not giuen cure to the same. For our chiefe Surgeon being dead, and the other absent by the losse of our vice-admirall, and hauing none left vs but a boy, whose good will was more then any skill hee had, we were little better then altogether destitute of such cunning and helpes as so grieuous a state of so many wounded bodies did require. Notwithstanding God, by the good aduice of our Generall, and the diligent putting too of euery mans helpe, did giue such speedy and wonderfull cure, that we had all great comfort thereby, and yeelded God the glory thereof.

The cause of this force and iniurie by these Ilanders, was no other but the deadly hatred which they beare against their cruell enemies the Spaniards, for the bloudy and most tirannous oppression which they had vsed towards them. And therefore with purpose against them (suspecting vs to bee Spaniards indeed, and that the rather, by occasion that though command was giuen to the contrary, some of our men in demanding water, vsed the Spanish word *Aqua*) sought some part of reuenge against vs.

Our Generall notwithstanding he might haue reuenged this wrong, with little hazard or danger; yet being more desirous to preserue one of his owne men aliue, then to destroy 100. of his

enemies,

enemies, committed the same to God: wishing this onely punishment to them, that they did but know whom they had wronged; and that they had done this iniurie not to an enemie, but to a friend; not to a Spaniard, but to an Engl.shman; who would rather haue beene a patron to defend them, then any way an instrument of the leastwrong that should haue beene done vnto them. The weapons which this people vse in their warres, are arrowes of reeds, with heads of stone, very brittle and indented, but darts of a great length, headed with iron or bone.

The same day that we receiued this dangerous affront, in the afternoone we set sayle from thence: and because we were now nigh the appointed height, wherein our ships were to be looked for, as also the extremity and crasie state of our hurt men aduising vs to vse expedition, to finde some conuenient place of repose, which might afford them some rest, and yeeld vs necessary supply of fresh victuals for their diet; we bent our course, as the wind would suffer vs, directly to run in with the maine. Where falling with a bay, called *Philips Bay*, in 32. deg. or thereabout, Nouemb. 30. we came to anchor: and foorthwith manned and *Nou.*30. sent our boate to discouer what likelihood the place would offer to affoord vs such things as we stood in need of.

Our boate doing her vttermost endeuour in a diligent search, yet after long trauell could find no appearance of hope for reliefe, either of fresh victuals or of fresh water: huge heards of wild buffes they might discerne, but not so much as any signe of any inhabitant thereabout. Yet in their returne to vs, they descried within the bay, an Indian with his Canow as he was a fishing: him they brought aboard our generall, canow and all as he was in it. A comely personage, and of a goodly stature; his apparell was a white garment, reaching scarcely to his knees; his armes and legges were naked; his haire vpon his head verie long; without a beard, as all the Indians for the most part are. He seemed verie gentle, of mild and humble nature, being verie tractable to learne the vse of euery thing, and most gratefull for such things as our Generall bestowed vpon him. In him we might see

a moſt liuely patterne of the harmeleſſe diſpoſition of that people; and how grieuous a thing it is that they ſhould by any
meanes be ſo abuſed as all thoſe are, whom the Spaniards haue
any command or power ouer.

　　This man being courteouſly entertained, and his paines of
comming double requited; after we had ſhewed him, partly by
ſignes, and partly by ſuch things as we had, what things we needed, and would gladly receiue by his meanes, vpon exchange
of ſuch things as he would deſire; wee ſent him away with our
boate and his owne canow (which was made of reed ſtraw) to
land him where he would. Who being landed, and willing our
men to ſtay his returne, was immediatly met with by two or three
of his friends; to whom imparting his newes, and ſhewing what
gifts he had receiued, he gaue ſo great content, that they willingly furthered his purpoſe; ſo that, after certaine houres of our
mens abode there, hee with diuers others (among whom was
their head or Captaine) made their returne; bringing with them
their loadings of ſuch things as they thought would do vs good:
as ſome hennes, egges, a fat hogge, and ſuch like. All which
(that our men might be without all ſuſpition of all euill to be
meant or intended by them) they ſent in one of their canowes,
a reaſonable diſtance from off the ſhoare, to our boate, the ſea-
gate being at that preſent very great, and their Captaine hauing
ſent backe his horſe, would needs commit himſelfe to the credit
of our men, though ſtrangers, and come with them to our Generall, without any of his owne acquaintance or countriemen
with him.

　　By his comming as we vnderſtood, that there was no meane
or way, to haue our neceſſities relieued in this place; ſo he offered himſelfe to be our pilote, to a place and that a good harborough, not farre backe to the Southward againe: where, by
way of traffique, we might haue at pleaſure, both water, and
thoſe other things which we ſtood in need of. This offer our generall very gladly receiued, and ſo much the rather, for that the
place intended, was neere about the place appointed, for the

rande-

randeuoues of our fleete. Omitting therefore our purpose, of pursuing the buffes formerly spoken of, of which we had otherwise determined, if possible to haue killed some; this good newes of better prouision, and more easie to come by, drew vs away: and so the 5. day after our arriuall, viz. December 4. we departed hence, and the next day December 5. by the willing conduct of our new Indian Pilote, we came to anchor in the desired harbor.

This harbor the Spaniards call *valperizo*, and the towne adioyning *Saint Iames* of *Chinli* it stands in 35. deg. 40. min. where albeit we neither met with our ships, nor heard of them, yet there was no good thing which the place afforded, or which our necessities indeed for the present required, but we had the same in great abundance: amongst other things we found in the towne diuerse storehouses of the wines of *Chilie*; and in the harbour, a ship called the *Captaine of Moriall, or the grand Captaine of the South, Admirall to the Ilands of Salomon*; loaden for the most part, with the same kinde of liquors: onely there was besides, a certaine quantity of fine gold of Baldiuia and a great crosse of gold beset with Emeraulds, on which was nailed a God of the same mettall, wee spent some time in refreshing our selues, and easing this ship of so heauy a burthen: and on the 8. day of the same moneth(hauing in the meane time, sufficiently stored our selues with necessaries, as wine, bread, bacon &c. for a long season)we set saile, returning backe towards the line; carrying againe our Indian pilote with vs, whom our generall bountifully rewarded, and enriched with many good things, which pleased him exceedingly, and caused him, by the way, to be landed in the place where he desired.

Our necessities being thus to our content releeued, our next care was the regaining(if possible)of the company of our ships, so long seuered from vs: neither would any thing haue satisfied our generall, or vs so well, as the happy meeting, or good newes of them, this way therefore(all other thoughts for the present set apart)were all our studies and endeauours bent, how to fit it

so,

so, as that no opportunity of meeting them might be passed ouer.

To this end, considering that we could not conueniently runne in with our ship(in search of them)to euery place, where was likelihood of being a harbour; and that our boate was too little, and vnable to carry men enough, to encounter the malice or treachery of the Spaniards(if we should by any chance meete with any of them)who are vsed to shew no mercy, where they may ouermaster; and therefore meaning not to hazard our selues to their cruell courtesie; we determined, as we coasted now towards the line, to search diligently for some conuenient place, where we might, in peace and safety, stay the trimming of our ship, and the erecting of a pinnace, in which wee might with better security, then in our boate, and without endangering of our ship, by running into each creeke, leaue no place vntried, if happily we might so finde againe our friends and countrimen.

Dec. 19.   For this cause December 19. we entred a bay, not farre to the Southward of the towne of Cyppo now inhabited by the Spaniards, in 29. deg. 30. min. where hauing landed certaine of our men, to the number of 14. to search what conueniency the place was likely to afford, for our abiding there; we were immediatly descried by the Spaniards, of the towne of Cyppo, aforesayd, who speedily made out 300. men at least wherof 100. were Spaniards, euery one well mounted vpon his horse; the rest were Indians, running as dogs, at their heeles, all naked, and in most miserable bondage.

They could not come any way so closely, but God did open our eyes to see them, before there was any extremity of danger, whereby our men being warned, had reasonable time to shift themselues as they could; first from the maine, to a rocke within the sea; and from thence into their boate: which being ready to receiue them, conueighed them with expedition, out of the reach of the Spaniards fury, without the hurt of any man.

Onely one *Richard Mininy*, being ouer bold and carelesse of
his

his owne safety, would not be intreated by his friends, nor feared by the multitude of his enemies, to take the present benefit of his owne deliuery : but chofe either to make 300. mē by outbrauing of them to become afraide, or elfe himfelfe to die in the place; the latter of which indeed he did, whofe dead body being drawne by the Indians from the rocke to the fhoare, was there manfully by the Spaniards beheaded, the right hand cut off, the heart pluckt out, all which they carried away in our fight, and for the reft of his carcafe, they caufed the Indians to fhoote it full of arrowes, made but the fame day, of greene wood, and fo left it to be deuoured of the beaftes and foules but that we went afhoare againe and buried it : wherein as there appeareth a moft extreame and barbarous cruelty, fo doth it declare to the world, in what miferable feare the Spaniard holdeth the gouernment of thofe parts; liuing in continuall dread of forreigne inuafion by ftrangers, or fecret cutting of their throats, by thofe whom they kept vnder them in fo fhamefull flauery, I meane the innocent and harmeleffe Indians. And therefore they make fure to murther what ftrangers foeuer they can come by, and fuffer the Indians by no meanes to haue any weapon longer then they be in prefent feruice : as appeared by their arrowes cut from the tree the fame day, as alfo by the credible report of others who knew the matter to be true. Yea they fuppofe they fhew the wretches great fauour, when they do not for their pleafures whip them with cords, and day by day drop their naked bodies with burning bacon : which is one of the leaft cruelties, amongft many, which they vniuerfally vfe againft that Nation and people.

This being not the place we looked for, nor the entertainement fuch as we defired; we fpeedily got hence againe, and Decemb. 20. the next day, fell with a more conuenient harbour, in a bay fomewhat to the Northward of the forenamed *Cyppo*, lying in 27. deg. 55. min. South the line.

Dec. 20.

In this place we fpent fome time in trimming of our fhip, and building of our pinnace, as we defired: but ftill the griefe for the

H   abfence

abſence of our friends remained with vs, for the finding of
whom, our generall hauing now fitted all things to his mind, intended (leauing his ſhip the meane while at anchor in the bay)
with his pinnace and ſome choſen men, himſelfe to returne
backe to the Southwards againe; to ſee if happily he might either himſelfe meete with them, or find them in ſome harbour, or
creeke; or heare of them by any others, whom he might meete
with, with this reſolution he ſet on, but after one daies ſayling,
the winde being contrary to his purpoſe, he was forced, whether
he would or no to returne againe.

within this bay, during our abode there, we had ſuch abundance of fiſh, not much vnlike our Gurnard in England, as no
place had euer afforded vs the like (Cape Blanck onely vpon
the coaſt of Barbary excepted) ſince our firſt ſetting forth of
Plymmouth, vntill this time, the plenty whereof in this place
was ſuch, that our gentlemen ſporting themſelues day by day,
with 4. or 5. hookes and lines, in 2. or 3. houres, would take
ſometimes 400. ſometimes more at one time.

All our buſineſſes being thus diſpatched, Ianuary 19. we ſet
Ian. 19. ſayle from hence; and the next place that we fell withall, Ian.
*Ian.*22. 22. was an Iland ſtanding in the ſame height, with the North
cape of the prouince of Mormorena, at this Iland we found 4.
Indians with their canowes, which tooke vpon them to bring
our men to a place of freſh water, on the foreſayd cape; in hope
whereof, our generall made them great cheere (as his manner
was towards all ſtrangers) and ſet his courſe by their direction,
but when we came vnto the place, and had trauelled vp a long
way into the land, wee found freſh water indeed, but ſcarce ſo
much as they had drunke wine in their paſſage thither.

As we ſayled along, continually ſearching for freſh water;
we came to a place called Tarapaca, and landing there we lighted on a Spaniard who lay aſleepe, and had lying by him 13.
barres of ſiluer, waighing in all, about 4000. Spaniſh duccatts:
wewould not (could wee haue choſen) haue awaked him of his
nappe: but ſeeing we, againſt our wills, did him that iniury, we
freed

freed him of his charge, which otherwise perhaps would haue kept him waking, and so left him to take out (if it pleased him) the other part of his sleepe, in more securitie.

Our search for water still continuing, as we landed againe not farre from thence, we met a Spaniard with an Indian boy, driuing 8. Lambes or Peruvian sheepe: each sheepe bare two leathren bagges, and in each bagge was 50. pound waight of refined siluer, in the whole 800. waight: we could not indure to see a gentleman Spaniard turnd carrier so; and therefore without intreaty, we offered our seruice, and became drouers: onely his directions were not so perfect, that we could keepe the way which hee intended; for almost as soone as hee was parted from vs, we with our new kinde of carriges, were come vnto our boates.

Farther beyond this cape fore-mentioned lie certaine Indian towns, frō whence as we passed by, came many of the people in certaine bawses made of Seales skins; of which two being ioyned together of a iust length, and side by side, resemble in fashion or forme a boate: they haue in either of them a small gutt, or some such thing blowne full of winde; by reason whereof it floateth, and is rowed very swiftly, carrying in it no small burthen. In these vpon sight of our ship, they brought store of fish of diuerse sortes, to traffique with vs, for any trifles wee would giue them: as kniues, margarites, glasses, and such like, whereof, men of 60. & 70. yeares old, were as glad as if they had receiued some exceeding rich commodity; being a most simple and plaine dealing people. Their resort vnto vs was such, as considering the shortnesse of the time, was wonderfull to vs to behold.

Not farre from this, viz. in 22. deg. 30. min. lay Mormorena, another great towne of the same people, ouer whom 2. Spaniards held the gouerment, with these our generall thought meet to deale; or at least to try their courtesy, whether they would, in way of traffique, giue vs such things as we needed or no, and therefore Ian. the 26. we cast anchor here, we found them (more *Ian. 26.*

H 2   for

for feare then for loue) somewhat tractable , and receiued from them by exchange many good things , very necessarie for our vses.

Amongst other things which we had of them , the sheepe of the countrey (viz. such as we mentioned before bearing the leatherne bags) were most memorable. Their height and length was equall to a pretty cow, and their strength fully answerable, if not by much exceeding their size or stature. Vpon one of their backes did sit at one time three well growne and tall men , and one boy, no mans foot touching the ground by a large foot in length , the beast nothing at all complaining of his burthen in the meane time. These sheepe haue neckes like camels ; their heads bearing a reasonable resemblance of another sheepe. The Spaniards vse them to great profit. Their wooll is exceeding fine, their flesh good meate, their increase ordinarie , and besides they supply the roome of horses for burthen or trauell: yea they serue to carry ouer the mountaines, maruellous loades, for 300. leagues together, where no other carriage can be made but by them onely. Hereabout, as also all along, and vp into the countrey throughout the Prouince of Cusko , the common ground wheresoeuer it bee taken vp , in euery hundred pound weight of earth, yeeldeth 25. s. of pure siluer, after the rate of a crowne an ounce.

The next place likely to affoord vs any newes of our ships (for in all this way from the height where wee builded our pinnace, there was no bay or harbour at all for shipping) was the port of the towne of Arica, standing in 20. deg. whither we arri-
ued the 7. of February. This towne seemed to vs to stand in the most fruitfull soile that we saw all alongst these coasts:both for that it is situate in the mouth of a most pleasant and fertile vally, abounding with all good things; as also in that it hath continuall trade of shipping, as well from Lyma as from all other parts of Peru. It is inhabited by the Spaniards. In two barks here, we found some forty and odde barres of siluer (of the bignesse and fashion of a brickbatte , and in waight each of them about 20.
                                                            pounds)

pounds) of which wee tooke the burthen on our selues to ease them, and so departed towards Chowley ; with which wee fell the second day following, viz. Febr. 9. and in our way to *Lima,* we met with another barke at *Ariquipa,* which had begun to loade some siluer and gold, but hauing had (as it seemed from Arica by land) some notice of our comming, had vnloaden the same againe before our arriuall. Yet in this our passage we met another barke loaden with linnen : some of which we thought might stand vs in some stead, and therefore tooke it with vs.

At Lima we arriued Febr. 15, and notwithstanding the Spa- niards forces, though they had thirtie ships at that present in harbour there, whereof 17. (most of them the especiall ships in all the South sea) were fully ready, we entred and anchored all night in the middest of them, in the Calao : and might haue made more spoile amongst them in few houres if we had beene affected to reuenge, then the Spaniard could haue recouered againe in many yeares. But wee had more care to get vp that company which we had so long mist, then to recompence their cruell and hard dealing by an euen requitall, which now wee might haue tooke. This Lima stands in 12. deg. 30. min. South latitude.

Here albeit no good newes of our ships could bee had, yet got we the newes of some things that seemed to comfort, if not to counteruaile our trauells thither, as namely, that in the ship of one *Mighell Angell* there, there were 1500. barres of plate, besides some other things (as silkes, linnen, and in one a chest full of royals of plate) which might stand vs in some stead in the other ships ; aboard whom we made somewhat bold to bid our selues welcome. Here also we heard the report of some things that had befallen in & neere Europe, since our departure thence; In particular of the death of some great personages : as, the king of Portugall, and both the kings of Morocco and Fesse, dead all three in one day at one battell : The death of the king of France, and the Pope of Rome : Whose abhominations as they are in part cut off from some Christian kingdomes, where his shame

is

is manifeſt,ſo do his vaſſals and accurſed inſtruments labour by all meanes poſſible to repaire that loſſe , by ſpreading the ſame the further in theſe parts, where his diuelliſh illuſions and damnable deceiuings are not knowne. And as his doctrine takes place any where, ſo do the manners that neceſſarily accompanie the ſame inſinuate themſelues together with the doctrine. For as its true that in all the parts of America, where the Spaniards haue any gouernment, the poiſonous infection of Popery hath ſpread it ſelfe; ſo on the other ſide it is as true, that there is no Citie, as Lima, Panama, Mexico,&c. no towne or village, yea no houſe almoſt in all theſe Prouinces, wherein (amongſt other the like Spaniſh vertues) not onely whoredome, but the filthineſſe of Sodome, not to bee named among Chriſtians, is not common without reproofe : the Popes pardons being more rife in theſe parts then they be in any part of Europe, for theſe filthineſſes whereout he ſucketh no ſmall aduantage. Notwithſtanding the Indians, who are nothing neerer the true knowledge of God then they were afore , abhorre this moſt filthie and loathſome manner of liuing; Shewing themſelues in reſpect of the Spaniards, as the Scythians did in reſpect of the Grecians: who in their barbarous ignorance, yet in life and behauiour did ſo farre excell the wiſe and learned Greekes, as they were ſhort of them in the gifts of learning and knowledge.

But as the Pope and Antichriſtian Biſhops labour by their wicked factors with tooth and naile to deface the glory of God, and to ſhut vp in darkneſſe the light of the Goſpell; ſo God doth not ſuffer his name and Religion to be altogether without witneſſe, to the reprouing both of his falſe and damnable doctrine, as alſo crying out againſt his vnmeaſurable and abhominable licentiouſneſſe of the fleſh, euen in theſe parts. For in this City of Lima, not two monethes before our comming thither , there were certaine perſons , to the number of twelue apprehended, examined, and condemned for the profeſſion of the Goſpell, and reprouing the doctrines of men, with the filthie manners vſed in that City: Of which twelue, ſixe were bound to one ſtake

and

and burnt, the reſt remained yet in priſon, to drinke of the ſame   1578.
cup within few dayes. Laſtly, here we had intelligence of a certaine rich ſhip, which was loaden with gold and ſiluer for Panama, that had ſet forth of this hauen the ſecond of February.

The very next day therefore in the morning (viz. the 16. of *Feb.* 16.
the ſaid moneth) wee ſet ſayle, as long as the wind would ſerue
our turne, and towed our ſhip as ſoone as the wind failed; continuing our courſe toward Panama, making ſtay no where, but
haſtening all wee might, to get ſight if it were poſſible, of that
gallant ſhip the *Cacafuego*, the great glory of the South ſea;
which was gone from Lima 14. dayes before vs.

We fell with the port of Paita in 4. deg. 40. min. Feb. 20. with *Febr.* 20.
port Saint *Hellen* and the riuer and port of Guiaquill, Febr. 24. *Febr.* 24.
we paſt the line the 28. and the firſt of March wee fell with cape *Febr.* 28.
Franciſco : where, about midday, we deſcried a ſayle a head of *March* 1.
vs, with whom after once we had ſpoken with her, we lay ſtill in
the ſame place about ſixe dayes ; to recouer our breath againe
which we had almoſt ſpent with haſty following, and to recall
to mind what aduentures had paſt vs ſince our late comming
from Lima; but eſpecially to do *Iohn de Anton* a kindneſſe, in
freeing him of the care of thoſe things with which his ſhip was
loaden.

This ſhip we found to bee the ſame of which we had heard,
not onely in the Calao of Lima, but alſo by diuers occaſions
afterward (which now we are at leaſure to relate, viz. by a ſhip
which we tooke betweene Lima and Paita : by another which
we took loaden with wine in the port of Paita: by a third loaden
with tackling and implements for ſhips (beſides eightie pound
waight in gold) from Guiaquill. And laſtly, by *Gabriel Aluarez*,
with whom we talked ſomewhat neerer the line) we found her
to be indeed the *Cacafuego* : though before we left her, ſhe were
new named by a boy of her owne the *Cacaplata.* We found in
her ſome fruite, conſerues, ſugars, meale and other victuals, and
(that which was the eſpecialleſt cauſe of her heauy and ſlow
ſayling) a certaine quantitie of iewels and precious ſtones, 13.
                                                      ch eſts

chests of ryals of plate; 80. pound waight in gold; 26. tunne of vncoyned siluer; two very faire gilt siluer drinking boules, and the like trifles, valued in all at about 360000. pezoes. We gaue the master a little linnen and the like, for these commodities; and at the end of sixe dayes we bad farewell and parted. Hee hastening somewhat lighter then before to Panama, we ply-ing off to sea, that we might with more leasure consider what course hence forward were fittest to be taken.

And considering that now we were come to the Northward of the line *(Cape Francisco* standing in the entrance of the bay of Panama, in 1. deg. of North latitude) and that there was no likelihood or hope that our ships should be before vs that way by any meanes: seeing that in running so many degrees from the Southermost Ilãds hitherto, we could not haue any signe or no-tice of their passage that way, notwithstanding that we had made so diligent search, and carefull enquirie after them, in euery har-bour or creeke almost as we had done; and considering also that the time of the yeare now drew on, wherein we must attempt, or of necessitie wholly giue ouer that action which chiefly our Ge-nerall had determined : namely, the discouery of what passage there was to be found, about the Northerne parts of America, from the South sea, into our owne Ocean(which being once discouered, and made knowne to be nauigable, we should not onely do our countrie a good and notable seruice, but we also our selues, should haue a neerer cut and passage home : where otherwise, we were to make a very long and tedious voyage of it, which would hardly agree with our good liking, we hauing beene so long from home already, and so much of our strength seperated from vs)which could not at all be done, if the oppor-tunity of time were now neglected : we therefore all of vs wil-lingly harkened, and consented to our generalls aduice : which was, first to seeke out some conuenient place, wherein to trimme our ship, and store our selues with wood and water and other prouisions, as we could get : and thenceforward to hasten on our intended journey, for the discouery of the said passage,
                                                              through

through which we might with joy returne to our longed homes.

From this cape before we set onward March the 7. shaping our course towards the Iland of *Caines*, with which we fell March 16. setling our selues for certaine dayes, in a fresh riuer, betweene the maine and it; for the finishing of our needfull businesses as it is aforesaid. While we abode in this place, we felt a very terrible earthquake, the force whereof was such, that our ship and pinnace, riding very neere an English mile from the shoare, were shaken and did quiuer as if it had beene layd on drie land : we fonnd here many good commodities which wee wanted, as fish, fresh water, wood &c. besides Alagartoes, Munckeyes and the like, and in our iourny hither, we met with one ship more(the latt wee met with in all those coastes)loaden with linnen, China-silke and China-dishes, amongst which wee found also a Faulcon of gold, handsomly wrought, with a great emerald set in the brest of it.

From hence we parted the 24. day of the moneth forenamed, with full purpose to runne the neerest course, as the winde would suffer vs, without touch of land a long time; and therefore passed by port Papagaia; the port of the Vale, of the most rich and excellent balmes of Iericho; Quantapico; and diuerse others : as also certaine gulphes hereabouts, which without intermission, send forth such continuall and violent windes, that the Spaniards, though their ships be good, dare not venture themselues too neere the danger of them.

Notwithstanding, hauing notice that we should be troubled with often calmes, and contrary windes, if we cotinued neere the coast, and did not runne of to sea to fetch the winde; and that if we did so, we could not then fall with land againe when we would: our generall thought it needfull, that we should runne in with some place or other, before our departure from the coast; to see if happily wee could, by traffique, augment our prouision of victuals, and other necessaries : that being at sea, we might not be driuen to any great want or necessi-

I　　tie

1578.

tie, albeit wee had reaſonable ſtore of good things aboard vs already.

Apr. 15.

The next harbor therefore which we chanced with, on April 15. in 15. deg. 40. min. was Guatulco ſo named of the Spaniards who inhabited it, with whom we had ſome entercourſe, to the ſupply of many things which we deſired, and chiefely bread &c. And now hauing reaſonably, as wee thought prouided our ſelues, we departed from the coaſt of America for the preſent: but not forgetting, before we gate a-ſhipboard, to take with vs alſo a certaine pot (of about a buſhell in bigneſſe) full of ryalls of plate, which we found in the towne: together with a chaine of gold, and ſome other iewells, which we intreated a gentleman Spaniard to leaue behinde him, as he was flying out of towne.

Apr. 16.

From Guatulco we departed the day following, viz. Aprill 16. ſetting our courſe directly into the ſea: whereon we ſayled 500. leagues in longitude, to get a winde: and betweene that and Iune 3. 1400. leagues in all, till we came into 42. deg. of North latitude, where in the night following, we found ſuch alteration of heate, into extreame and nipping cold, that our men in generall, did grieuouſly complaine thereof; ſome of them feeling their healths much impaired thereby, neither was it, that this chanced in the night alone, but the day following carried with it, not onely the markes, but the ſtings and force of the night going before; to the great admiration of vs all, for beſides that the pinching and biting aire, was nothing altered; the very roapes of our ſhip were ſtiffe, and the raine which fell, was an vnnatural congealed and frozen ſubſtance, ſo that we ſeemed rather to be in the frozen Zone, then any way ſo neere vnto the ſun, or theſe hotter climates.

Neither did this happen for the time onely, or by ſome ſudden accident, but rather ſeemes indeed, to proceed from ſome ordinary cauſe, againſt the which the heate of the ſun preuailes not, for it came to that extremity, in ſayling but 2. deg. farther to the Northward in our courſe: that though ſea-men lack not

good

good ftomaches, yet it feemed a queftion to many amongft vs, whether their hands fhould feed their mouthes, or rather keepe themfelues within their couerts, from the pinching cold that did benumme them. Neither could we impute it to the tender-neffe of our bodies, though we came lately from the extremitie of heate, by reafon whereof we might be more fenfible of the prefent cold: infomuch as the dead and fenceleffe creatures, were as well affected with it as our felues, our meate as foone as it was remooued from the fire, would prefently in a manner be frozen vp; and our ropes and tackling, in few dayes were growne to that ftiffeneffe, that what 3. men afore were able with them to performe, now 6. men with their beft ftrength, and vttermoft endeauour, were hardly able to accomplifh: whereby a fudden and great difcouragement feafed vpon the mindes of our men, and they were poffeffed with a great mif-like, and doubtiug of any good to be done that way, yet would not our general be difcouraged, but as wel by comfortable fpee ches, of the diuine prouidence, and of Gods louing care ouer his children, out of the fcriptures; as alfo by other good and profitable perfwafions, adding thereto his own cheerfull exam-ple, he fo ftirred them vp, to put on a good courage, and to quite themfelues like men, to indure fome fhort extremity, to haue the fpeedier comfort, and a little trouble, to obtaine the greater glory; that euery man was throughly armed with wil-lingneffe, and refolued to fee the vttermoft, if it were poffible, of what good was to be done that way.

The land in that part of America, bearing farther out into the Weft, then we before imagined, we were neerer on it then wee were aware; and yet the neerer ftill wee came vnto it, the more extremitie of cold did feafe vpon vs. The 5. day of Iune, *Iune* 5. wee were forced by contrary windes, to run in with the fhoare, which we then firft defcried; and to caft anchor in a bad bay, the beft roade we could for the prefent meete with: where wee were not without fome danger, by reafon of the many extreme gufts, and flawes that beate vpon vs; which if they ceafed and were still at any time, immediatly vpon their intermission, there followed most vile, thicke, and stinking fogges; against which the sea preuailed nothing, till the gusts of wind againe remoued them, which brought with them, such extremity and violence when they came, that there was no dealing or resisting against them.

In this place was no abiding for vs; and to go further North, the extremity of the cold (which had now vtterly discouraged our men) would not permit vs : and the winds directly bent against vs, hauing once gotten vs vnder sayle againe, commanded vs to the Southward whether we would or no.

From the height of 48. deg. in which now we were, to 38. we found the land by coasting alongst it to bee but low and reasonable plaine : euery hill (whereof we saw many, but none verie high) though it were in Iune, and the Sunne in his neerest approch vnto them being couered with snow.

In 38 deg. 30. min. we fell with a conuenient and fit harborough, and Iune 17. came to anchor therein. : where we continued till the 23. day of Iuly following. During all which time, notwithstanding it was in the height of Summer, and so neere the Sunne; yet were wee continually visited with like nipping colds, as we had felt before : insomuch that if violent exercises of our bodies, and busie imployment about our necessarie labours, had not sometimes compeld vs to the contrary, we could very well haue beene contented to haue kept about vs still our Winter clothes; yea (had our necessities suffered vs) to haue kept our beds; neither could we at any time in whole fourteene dayes together, find the aire so cleare as to be able to take the height of Sunne or starre.

And here hauing so fit occasion, (notwithstanding it may seeme to be besides the purpose of writing the history of this our voyage) we will a little more diligently inquire into the causes of the continuance of the extreame cold in these parts : as also into the probabilities or vnlikelihoods of a passage to be found that way. Neither was it (as hath formerly beene touched) the

tender-

tendernesse of our bodies, comming so lately out of the heate, whereby the poores were opened, that made vs so sensible of the colds we here felt: in this respect, as in many others, we found our God a prouident father, and carefull Physitian for vs. We lacked no outward helpes nor inward comforts, to restore and fortifie nature, had it beene decayed or weakened in vs; neither was there wanting to vs the great experience of our Generall, who had often himselfe proued the force of the burning Zone; whose aduice alwayes preuailed much to the preseruing of a moderate temper in our constitutions: so that euen after our departure from the heate wee alwayes found our bodies not as sponges, but strong and hardned, more able to beare out cold, though we came out of excesse of heate, then a number of chamber champions could haue beene, who lye on their feather-beds till they go to sea, or rather whose teeth in a temperate aire do beate in their heads, at a cup of cold Sack and sugar by the fire.

And that it was not our tendernes, but the very extremitie of the cold it selfe, that caused this sensiblenes in vs, may the rather appeare in that the naturall inhabitants of the place (with whom we had for a long season familiar intercourse, as is to be related) who had neuer beene acquainted with such heate; to whom the countrey, ayre, and climate was proper; and in whom custome of cold was as it were a second nature: yet vsed to come shiuering to vs in their warme furres; crowding close together body to body, to receiue heate one of another; and sheltring themselues vnder a lee bancke, if it were possible; and as often as they could, labouring to shroude themselues vnder our garments also, to keepe them warme. Besides how vnhandsome and deformed appeared the face of the earth it selfe! shewing trees without leaues, and the ground without greennes in those moneths of Iune and Iuly. The poore birds and foules not daring (as we had great experience to obserue it) not daring so much as once to arise from their nests, after the first egge layed, till it with all the rest be hatched, and brought to some strength of nature, able to helpe it selfe. Onely this recompence hath nature affoorded

I 3   them,

them, that the heate of their owne bodies being exceeding great, it perfecteth the creature with greater expedition, and in shorter time then is to be found in many other places.

As for the causes of this extremity they seeme not to be so deeply hidden, but that they may at least in part be guessed at: The chiefest of which we conceiue to be the large spreading of the Asian and American continent, which (somewhat North-ward of these parts) if they be not fully-ioyned, yet seeme they to come very neere one to the other. From whose high and snow-couered mountaines, the North and North west winds (the constant visitants of those coasts) send abroad their frozen nimphes, to the infecting of the whole aire with this insufferable sharpnesse : not permitting the Sunne, no not in the pride of his heate, to dissolue that congealed matter and snow, which they haue breathed out so nigh the Sunne, and so many degrees distant from themselues. And that the North and North-west winds are here constant in Iune and Iuly, as the North wind a-lone is in August and September; we not onely found it by our owne experience, but were fully confirmed in the opinion there-of, by the continued obseruations of the Spaniards. Hence comes the generall squalidnesse and barrennesse of the countrie; hence comes it, that in the middest of their Summer, the snow hardly departeth euen from their very doores, but is neuer ta-ken away from their hils at all; hence come those thicke mists and most stinking fogges, which increase so much the more, by how much higher the pole is raised : wherein a blind pilot is as good as the best director of a course. For the Sunne striuing to performe his naturall office, in eleuating the vapors out of these inferior bodies, draweth necessarily abundance of moisture out of the sea: but the nipping cold (from the former causes) mee-ting and opposing the Sunnes indeuour, forces him to giue ouer his worke imperfect : and instead of higher eleuation, to leaue in the lowest region, wandring vpon the face of the earth and wa-ters, as it were a second sea: through which its owne beames can-not possibly pierce, vnlesse sometimes when the sudden violence

of

of the winds doth helpe to scatter and breake through it, which thing happeneth very seldome, and when it happeneth is of no continuance. Some of our marriners in this voyage had formerly beene at Wardhouse, in 72. deg. of North latitude: who yet affirmed, that they felt no such nipping cold there in the end of Summer, when they departed thence, as they did here in those hottest moneths of Iune and Iuly.

And also from these reasons we coniecture; that either there is no passage at all through these Northerne coasts (which is most likely) or if there be, that yet it is vnnauigable. Adde hereunto, that though we searched the coast diligently, euen vnto the 48. deg. yet found we not the land, to trend so much as one point in any place towards the East, but rather running on continually Northwest, as if it went directly to meet with Asia; and euen in that height when we had a franke wind, to haue carried vs through, had there beene a passage, yet we had a smooth and calme sea, with ordinary flowing and reflowing, which could not haue beene, had there beene a frete: of which we rather infallibly concluded then coniectured, that there was none. But to returne.

The next day after our comming to anchor in the aforesaid harbour, the people of the countrey shewed themselues; sending off a man with great expedition to vs in a canow. Who being yet but a little from the shoare, and a great way from our ship, spake to vs continually as he came rowing on. And at last at a reasonable distance staying himselfe, he began more solemnely a long and tedious oration, after his manner: vsing in the deliuerie thereof, many gestures and signes, mowing his hands, turning his head and body many wayes; and after his oration ended, with great shew of reuerence and submission, returned back to shoare againe. He shortly came againe the second time in like manner, and so the third time: When he brought with him (as a present from the rest) a bunch of feathers, much like the feathers of a blacke crow, very neatly and artificially gathered vpon a string, and drawne together into a round bundle; being verie

cleane

cleane and finely cut, and bearing in length an equall proportion one with another; a speciall cognizance (as wee afterwards obserued) which they that guard their kings person, weare on their heads. With this also he brought a little basket made of rushes, and filled with an herbe which they called *Tabáh*. Both which being tyed to a short rodde, he cast into our boate. Our Generall intended to haue recompenced him immediatly with many good things, he would haue bestowed vpon him : but entring into the boate to deliuer the same, he could not be drawne to receiue them by any meanes: saue one hat, which being cast into the water out of the ship, he tooke vp (refusing vtterly to meddle with any other thing, though it were vpon a board put off vnto him) and so presently made his returne. After which time, our boate could row no way, but wondring at vs as at gods, they would follow the same with admiration.

The 3. day following, viz. the 21. our ship hauing receiued a leake at sea, was brought to anchor neerer the shoare, that her goods being landed, she might be repaired : but for that we were to preuent any danger, that might chance against our safety, our generall first of all landed his men, with all necessary prouision, to build tents and make a fort for the defence of our selues and goods : and that wee might vnder the shelter of it, with more safety (what euer should befall) end our businesse; which when the people of the country perceiued vs doing, as men set on fire to war, in defence of their countrie, in great hast and companies, with such weapons as they had, they came downe vnto vs ; and yet with no hostile meaning, or intent to hurt vs: standing when they drew neere, as men rauished in their mindes, with the sight of such things as they neuer had seene, or heard of before that time : their errand being rather with submission and feare to worship vs as Gods, then to haue any warre with vs as with mortall men. Which thing as it did partly shew it selfe at that instant, so did it more and more manifest it selfe afterwards; during the whole time of our abode amongst them. At this time, being willed by signes to lay from

them

them their bowes and arrowes, they did as they were directed, and so did all the rest, as they came more and more by companies vnto them, growing in a little while, to a great number both of men and women.

To the intent therefore, that this peace which they themselues so willingly sought, might without any cause of the breach thereof, on our part giuen, be continued; and that wee might with more safety and expedition, end our businesses in quiet; our Generall with all his company, vsed all meanes possible, gently to intreate them, bestowing vpon each of them liberally, good and necessary things to couer their nakednesse, withall signifying vnto them, we were no Gods but men, and had neede of such things to couer our owne shame; teaching them to vse them to the same ends: for which cause also wee did eate and drinke in their presence, giuing them to vnderstand, that without that wee could not liue, and therefore were but men as well as they.

Notwithstanding nothing could perswade them, nor remoue that opinion, which they had conceiued of vs, that wee should be Gods.

In recompence of those things which they had receiued of vs, as shirts linnen cloth, &c. they bestowed vpon our generall, and diuerse of our company, diuerse things, as feathers, cawles of networke, the quiuers of their arrowes, made of fawne-skins, and the very skins of beasts that their women wore vpon their bodies. Hauing thus had their fill of this times visiting and beholding of vs, they departed with ioy to their houses, which houses are digged round within the earth, and haue from the vppermost brimmes of the circle, clefts of wood set vp, and ioyned close together at the top, like our spires on the steeple of a Church: which being couered with earth, suffer no water to enter, and are very warme, the doore in the most part of them, performes the office also of a chimney, to let out the smoake: its made in bignesse and fashion, like to an ordinary scuttle in a ship, and standing slopewise: their beds are the hard ground,

K   onely

onely with ruſhes ſtrewed vpon it, and lying round about the houſe, haue their fire in the middeſt, which by reaſon that the houſe is but low vaulted, round and cloſe, giueth a maruelous reflexion to their bodies to heate the ſame.

Their men for the moſt part goe naked, the women take a-kinde of bulruſhes, and kembing it after the manner of hempe, make themſelues thereof a looſe garment, which being knitte a-bout their middles, hanges downe about their hippes, and ſo af-fordes to them a couering of that, which nature teaches ſhould be hidden: about their ſhoulders, they weare alſo the skin of a deere, with the haire vpon it. They are very obedient to their husbands, and exceeding ready in all ſeruices: yet of them-ſelues offring to do nothing, without the conſents, or being cal-led of the men.

As ſoone as they were rerurned to their houſes, they began a-mongſt themſelues a kind of moſt lamentable weeping & crying out; which they continued alſo a great while together, in ſuch ſort, that in the place where they left vs (being neere about 3. quarters of an Engliſh mile diſtant from them) we very plaine-ly, with wonder and admiration did heare the ſame: the women eſpecially, extending their voices, in a moſt miſerable and dole-full manner of ſhreeking.

Notwithſtanding this humble manner of preſenting them-ſelues, and awfull demeanour vſed towards vs, we thought it no wiſedome too farre to truſt them (our experience of former Infidels dealing with vs before, made vs carefull to prouide a-gainſt an alteration of their affections, or breach of peace if it ſhould happen) and therefore with all expedition we ſet vp our tents, and entrenched our ſelues with walls of ſtone: that ſo be-ing fortified within our ſelues, we might be able to keepe off the enemie (if they ſhould ſo proue) from comming amongſt vs without our good wills: this being quickly finiſhed we went the more cheerefully and ſecurely afterward, about our other buſineſſe.

Againſt the end of two daies (during which time they had

not

not againe beene with vs)there was gathered together a great affembly of men, women, and children(inuited by the report of them which firft faw vs, who as it feemes, had in that time, of purpofe difperfed themfelues into the country, to make knowne the newes)who came now the fecond time vnto vs, bringing with them as before had beene done, feathers and bagges of *To-bah* for prefents, or rather indeed for facrifices, vpon this perfwafion that we were Gods.

When they came to the top of the hill, at the bottome whereof wee had built our fort, they made a ftand; where one (appointed as their chiefe fpeaker) wearied both vs his hearers, and himfelfe too, with a long and tedious oration: deliuered with ftrange and violent geftures, his voice being extended to the vttermoft ftrength of nature, and his words falling fo thicke one in the neck of another, that he could hardly fetch his breath againe: as foone as he had concluded, all the reft, with a reuerend bowing of their bodies(in a dreaming manner, and long producing of the fame)cryed *Oh*: thereby giuing their confents, that all was very true which he had fpoken, and that they had vttered their minde by his mouth vnto vs; which done, the men laying downe their bowes vpon the hill, and leauing their women and children behinde them, came downe with their prefents; in fuch fort, as if they had appeared before a God indeed: thinking themfelues happy, that they might haue acceffe vnto our generall, but much more happy, when they fawe that he would receiue at their hands, thofe things which they fo willingly had prefented: and no doubt, they thought themfelues neereft vnto God, when they fate or ftood next to him: In the meane time the women, as if they had beene defperate, vfed vnnaturall violence againft themfelues, crying and fhrecking piteoufly, tearing their flefh with their nailes from their cheekes, in a monftrous manner, the blood ftreaming downe along their brefts; befides defpoiling the vpper parts of their bodies, of thofe fingle couerings they formerly had, and holding their hands aboue their heads, that they might not refcue their brefts

K 2　　　　　　　　　　　from

from harme, they would with furie caſt themſelues vpon the
ground, neuer reſpecting whether it were cleane or ſoft, but
daſhed themſelues in this manner on hard ſtones, knobby, hil-
locks, ſtocks of wood, and pricking buſhes, or what euer elſe lay
in their way, itterating the ſame courſe againe and againe : yea
women great with child, ſome nine or ten times each, and others
holding out till 15. or 16. times (till their ſtrengths failed them)
exerciſed this cruelty againſt themſelues: A thing more grieuous
for vs to ſee, or ſuffer could we haue holpe it, then trouble to
them (as it ſeemed) to do it.

This bloudie ſacrifice (againſt our wils) beeing thus performed, our Generall with his companie in the preſence of thoſe
ſtrangers fell to prayers : and by ſignes in lifting vp our eyes and
hands to heauen, ſignified vnto them, that that God whom we
did ſerue, and whom they ought to worſhip, was aboue: Beſee-
ching God if it were his good pleaſure to open by ſome meanes
their blinded eyes, that they might in due time be called to the
knowledge of him the true and euerliuing God, and of Ieſus
Chriſt whom he hath ſent, the ſaluation of the Gentiles. In the
time of which prayers, ſinging of Pſalmes, and reading of certaine Chapters in the Bible, they ſate very attentiuely : and ob-
ſeruing the end at euery pauſe, with one voice ſtill cryed, Oh,
greatly reioycing in our exerciſes. Yea they tooke ſuch pleaſure
in our ſinging of Pſalmes, that whenſoeuer they reſorted to vs,
their firſt requeſt was commonly this, *Gnaáh*, by which they intreated that we would ſing.

Our General hauing now beſtowed vpon them diuers things,
at their departure they reſtored them all againe ; none carrying
with him any thing of whatſoeuer hee had receiued, thinking
themſelues ſufficiently enriched and happie, that they had found
ſo free acceſſe to ſee vs.

Againſt the end of three daies more (the newes hauing the
while ſpread it ſelfe farther, and as it ſeemed a great way vp into
the countrie) were aſſembled the greateſt number of people,
which wee could reaſonably imagine, to dwell within any conuenient

uenient diftance round about. Amongft the reft, the king himfelfe, a man of a goodly ftature and comely perfonage, attended
with his guard, of about 100. tall and warlike men, this day, viz.
Iune 26. came downe to fee vs.

Before his comming, were fent two Embaffadors or meffen-
gers to our Generall, to fignifie that their *Hióh*, that is, their king
was comming and at hand. They in the deliuery of their meffage, the one fpake with a foft and low voice, prompting his fel-
low, the other pronounced the fame word by word after him,
with a voice more audible: continuing their proclamation (for
fuch it was) about halfe an houre. Which being ended, they by
fignes made requeft to our Generall, to fend fomething by their
hands to their *Hióh* or king, as a token that his comming might
be in peace. Our Generall willingly fatisfied their defire; and
they, glad men, made fpeedy returns to their *Hióh*. Neither was
it long before their king (making as princely a fhew as poffibly
he could) with all his traine came forward.

In their comming forwards they cryed continually after a
finging manner with a luftie courage. And as they drew neerer
and neerer towards vs, fo did they more and more ftriue to be-
haue themfelues with a certaine comelineffe and grauity in all
their actions.

In the forefront came a man of a large body and goodly af-
pect, bearing the Septer or royall mace (made of a certaine kind
of blacke wood, and in length about a yard and a halfe) before
the king. Whereupon hanged two crownes, a bigger and a leffe,
with three chaines of a maruellous length, and often doubled;
befides a bagge of the herbe *Tabáh*. The crownes were made of
knitworke, wrought vpon moft curioufly with feathers of diuers colours, very artificially placed, and of a formall fafhion:
The chaines feemed of a bony fubftance: euery linke or part
thereof being very little, thinne, moft finely burnifhed, with a
hole pierced through the middeft. The number of linkes going
to make one chaine, is in a manner infinite: but of fuch eftimation it is amongft them, that few be the perfons that are admit-

ted

ted to weare the fame: and euen they to whom its lawfull to vfe them, yet are ftinted what number they fhall vfe; as fome ten, fome twelue, fome twentie, and as they exceed in number of chaines, fo are they thereby knowne to be the more honorable perfonages.

Next vnto him that bare this Scepter, was the king himfelfe with his guard about him: His attire vpon his head was a cawle of knitworke, wrought vpon fomewhat like the crownes , but differing much both in fafhion and perfectneffe of worke; vpon his fhoulders he had on a coate of the skins of conies, reaching to his waft: His guard alfo had each coats of the fame fhape, but of other skins:fome hauing cawles likewife ftucke with feathers, or couered ouer with a certaine downe, which groweth vp in the countrey vpon an herbe much like our lectuce; which exceeds any other downe in the world for finenesse, and beeing layed vpon their cawles by no winds can be remoued: Of fuch eftimation is this herbe amongft them, that the downe thereof is not lawfull to be worne, but of fuch perfons as are about the king (to whom alfo it is permitted to weare a plume of feathers on their heads, in figne of honour) and the feeds are not vfed but onely in facrifice to their gods. After thefe in their order, did follow the naked fort of common people; whofe haire being long, was gathered into a bunch behind, in which ftucke plumes of feathers, but in the forepart onely fingle feathers like hornes, euery one pleafing himfelfe in his owne deuice.

This one thing was obferued to bee generall amongft them all; that euery one had his face painted, fome with white, fome blacke, and fome with other colours, euery man alfo bringing in his hand one thing or other for a gift or prefent: Their traine or laft part of their company confifted of women and children, each woman bearing againft her breaft a round basket or two, hauing within them diuers things, as bagges of *Tobáh*, a roote which they call *Petáh*, whereof they make a kind of meale, and either bake it into bread, or eate it raw; broyled fifhes like a pilchard; the feed and downe aforenamed, with fuch like:

Their

Their baskets were made in fashion like a deepe boale, and though the matter were rushes, or such other kind of stuffe, yet was it so cunningly handled, that the most part of them would hold water; about the brimmes they were hanged with peeces of the shels of pearles, and in some places with two or three linkes at a place, of the chaines forenamed : thereby signifying, that they were vessels wholly dedicated to the onely vse of the gods they worshipped: and besides this, they were wrought vppon with the matted downe of red feathers, distinguished into diuers workes and formes.

In the meane time our Generall hauing assembled his men together (as forecasting the danger, and worst that might fall out) prepared himselfe to stand vpon sure ground, that wee might at all times be ready in our owne defence, if any thing should chance otherwise then was looked for or expected.

Wherefore euery man being in a warlike readinesse, he marched within his fenced place, making against their approach a most warlike shew (as he did also at all other times of their resort) whereby if they had beene desperate enemies, they could not haue chosen but haue conceiued terrour and feare, with discouragement to attempt any thing against vs, in beholding of the same.

When they were come somewhat neere vnto vs, trooping together, they gaue vs a common or a generall salutation : obseruing in the meane time a generall silence. Whereupon he who bare the Scepter before the king, being prompted by another whom the king assigned to that office, pronounced with an audible and manly voice, what the other spake to him in secret: continuing, whether it were his oration or proclamation, at the least halfe an houre. At the close whereof, there was a common *Amen*, in signe of approbation giuen by euery person: And the king himselfe with the whole number of men and women (the little children onely remaining behind) came further downe the hill, and as they came set themselues againe in their former order.

And

And being now come to the foot of the hill and neere our fort, the Scepter bearer with a composed countenance and stately carriage began a song, and answerable thereunto, obserued a kind of measures in a dance: whom the king with his guard and euery other sort of person following, did in like manner sing and daunce, sauing onely the women who danced but kept silence. As they danced they still came on: and our Generall perceiuing their plaine and simple meaning, gaue order that they might freely enter without interruption within our bulwarke: Where after they had entred they yet continued their song and dance a reasonable time: their women also following them with their wassaile boales in their hands, their bodies bruised, their faces torne, their dugges, breasts, and other parts bespotted with bloud, trickling downe from the wounds, which with their nailes they had made before their comming.

After that they had satisfied or rather tired themselues in this manner, they made signes to our Generall to haue him sit down; Vnto whom both the king and diuers others made seuerall orations, or rather indeed if wee had vnderstood them, supplications, that hee would take the Prouince and kingdome into his hand, and become their king and patron: making signes that they would resigne vnto him their right and title in the whole land, and become his vassals in themselues and their posterities: Which that they might make vs indeed beleeue that it was their true meaning and intent; the king himselfe with all the rest with one consent, and with great reuerence, ioyfully singing a song, set the crowne vpon his head; inriched his necke with all their chaines; and offering vnto him many other things, honoured him by the name of *Hyóh.* Adding thereunto (as it might seeme) a song and dance of triumph: because they were not onely visited of the gods (for so they still iudged vs to be) but the great and chiefe god was now become their god, their king and patron, and themselues were become the onely happie and blessed people in all the world.

These things being so freely offered, our Generall thought
not

not meet to reiect or refuse the same: both for that he would not giue them any cause of mistruct, or disliking of him(that being the onely place, wherein at this present, we were of necessitie inforced to seeke reliefe of many things)and chiefely, for that he knew not to what good end God had brought this to passe, or what honour and profit it might bring to our countrie in time to come.

Wherefore in the name and to the vse of her most excellent maiesty, he tooke the scepter crowne and dignity, of the sayd countrie into his hand; wishing nothing more, then that it had layen so fitly for her maiesty to enioy, as it was now her proper owne, and that the riches and treasures thereof (wherewith in the vpland countries it abounds)might with as great conueniency be transported, to the enriching of her kingdome here at home, as it is in plenty to be attained there: and especially, that so tractable and louing a people, as they shewed themselues to be, might haue meanes to haue manifested their most willing obedience the more vnto her, and by her meanes, as a mother and nurse of the Church of *Christ*, might by the preaching of the Gospell, be brought to the right knowledge, and obedience of the true and euerliuing God.

The ceremonies of this resigning, and receiuing of the kingdome being thus performed, the common sort both of men and women, leauing the king and his guard about him, with our generall, dispersed themselues among our people, taking a diligent view or suruey of euery man; and finding such as pleased their fancies(which commonly were the youngest of vs)they presently enclosing them about, offred their sacrifices vnto them, crying out with lamentable shreekes and moanes, weeping, and scratching, and tearing their very flesh off their faces with their nailes, neither were it the women alone which did this, but euen old men, roaring and crying out, were as violent as the women were.

We groaned in spirit to see the power of Sathan so farre preuaile, in seducing these so harmelesse soules, and laboured by all

L meanes

means, both by shewing our great dislike, and when that serued not, by violent withholding of their hands from that madnesse, directing them (by our eyes and hands lift vp towards heauen) to the liuing God whom they ought to serue : but so mad were they vpon their Idolatry, that forcible withholding them wou d not preuaile (for as soone as they could get liberty to their hands againe, they would be as violent as they were before) till such time, as they whom they worshipped, were conueyed from them into the tents, whom yet as men besides themselues, they would with fury and outrage seeke to haue againe.

After that time had a little qualified their madnes, they then began to shew & make knowne vnto vs their griefes and diseases which they carried about them, some of them hauing old aches, some shruncke sinewes, some old soares and canckred vlcers, some wounds more lately receiued, and the like, in most lamentable manner crauing helpe and cure thereof from vs : making signes, that if we did but blowe vpon their griefes, or but touched the diseased places, they would be whole.

Their griefes we could not but take pitty on them, and to our power desire to helpe them : but that (if it pleased God to open their eyes) they might vnderstand we were but men and no gods, we vsed ordinary meanes, as, lotions, emplaisters, and vnguents most fitly (as farre as our skills could guesse) agreeing to the natures of their griefes, beseeching God, if it made for his glory, to giue cure to their diseases by these meanes. The like we did from time to time as they resorted to vs.

Few were the dayes, wherein they were absent from vs, during the whole time of our abode in that place : and ordinarily euery third day, they brought their sacrifices, till such time, as they certainely vnderstood our meaning, that we tooke no pleasure, but were displeased with them : whereupon their zeale abated, and their sacrificing, for a season, to our good liking ceased ; notwithstanding they continued still to make their resort vnto vs in great abundance, and in such sort, that they oft-times forgate, to prouide meate for their owne sustenance; so that
                                                                    our

our generall(of whom they made account as of a father)was
faine to performe the office of a father to them, relieuing them
with such victualls, as we had prouided for our selues, as, Muf-
cles, Seales, and such like, wherein they tooke exceeding much
content; and seeing that their sacrifices were displeasing to vs,
yet (hating ingratitude)they sought to recompence vs, with
such things as they had, which they willingly inforced vpon vs,
though it were neuer so necessarie or needfull for themselues to
keepe.

They are a people of a tractable, free,and louing nature,with-
out guile or treachery;their bowes and arrowes(their only weapons, and almost all their wealth)they vse very skillfully, but yet
not to do any great harme with them, being by reason of their
weakenesse, more fit for children then for men, sending the arrow neither farre off, nor with any great force : and yet are the
men commonly so strong of body, that that, which 2. or 3. of
our men could hardly beare, one of them would take vpon his
backe, and without grudging carrie it easily away, vp hill and
downe hill an English mile together: they are also exceeding
swift in running, and of long continuance; the vse whereof is so
familiar with them, that they seldome goe, but for the most
part runne. One thing we obserued in them with admiration :
that if at any time, they chanced to see a fish, so neere the shoare,
that they might reach the place without swimming, they would
neuer, or very seldome misse to take it.

After that our necessary businesses were well dispatched, our
generall with his gentlemen, and many of his company, made a
journy vp into the land, to see the manner of their dwelling,
and to be the better acquainted, with the nature and commodities of the country. Their houses were all such as wee haue for-
metly described, and being many of them in one place, made
seuerall villages here and there. The inland we found to be farre
different from the shoare, a goodly country, and fruitfull soyle,
stored with many blessings fit for the vse of man : infinite was
the company of very large and fat Deere, which there we sawe

by thouſands, as we ſuppoſed, in a heard: beſides a multitude of a ſtrange kinde of Conies, by farre exceeding them in number: their heads and bodies, in which they reſemble other Conies, are but ſmall; his tayle like the tayle of a Rat, exceeding long; and his feet like the pawes of a Want or Moale; vnder his chinne, on either ſide, he hath a bagge, into which he gathereth his meate, when he hath filled his belly abroade, that he may with it, either feed his young, or feed himſelfe, when he liſts not to trauaile from his burrough: the people eate their bodies, and make great account of their skinnes, for their kings holidaies coate was made of them.

This country our generall named *Albion*, and that for two cauſes; the one in reſpect of the white bancks and cliffes, which lie toward the ſea: the other, that it might haue ſome affinity, euen in name alſo, with our owne country, which was ſometime ſo called.

Before we went from thence, our generall cauſed to be ſet vp, a monument of our being there; as alſo of her maieſties, and ſucceſſors right and title to that kingdome, namely, a plate of braſſe, faſt nailed to a great and firme poſt; whereon is engrauen her graces name, and the day and yeare of our arriuall there, and of the free giuing vp, of the prouince and kingdome, both by the king and people, into her maieſties hands: together with her highneſſe picture, and armes in a piece of ſixpence currant Engliſh monie, ſhewing it ſelfe by a hole made of purpoſe through the plate: vnderneath was likewiſe engrauen the name of our generall &c.

The Spaniards neuer had any dealing, or ſo much as ſet a foote in this country; the vtmoſt of their diſcoueries, reaching onely to many degrees Southward of this place.

And now, as the time of our departure was perceiued by them to draw nigh, ſo did the ſorrowes and miſeries of this people, ſeeme to themſelues to increaſe vpon them; and the more certaine they were of our going away, the more doubtfull they ſhewed themſelues, what they might doe; ſo that we might eaſily fily iudge that that ioy (being exceeding great)wherewith they receiued vs at our firſt arriuall, was cleane drowned in their exceſſiue ſorrow for our departing: For they did not onely looſe on a ſudden all mirth, ioy, glad countenance, pleaſant ſpeeches, agility of body, familiar reioycing one with another, and all pleaſure whateuer fleſh and bloud might bee delighted in, but with ſighes and ſorrowings, with heauy hearts and grieued minds, they powred out wofull complaints and moanes, with bitter teares and wringing of their hands, tormenting themſelues. And as men refuſing all comfort, they onely accounted themſelues as caſt-awayes, and thoſe whom the gods were about to forſake: So that nothing we could ſay or do, was able to eaſe them of their ſo heauy a burthen, or to deliuer them from ſo deſperate a ſtraite, as our leauing of them did ſeeme to them that it would caſt them into.

Howbeit ſeeing they could not ſtill enioy our preſence, they (ſuppoſing vs to be gods indeed) thought it their duties to intreate vs that being abſent, we would yet be mindfull of them, and making ſignes of their deſires, that in time to come wee would ſee them againe, they ſtole vpon vs a ſacrifice, and ſet it on fire erre we were aware; burning therein a chaine and a bunch of feathers. We laboured by all meanes poſſible to withhold or withdraw them but could not preuaile, till at laſt we fell to prayers and ſinging of Pſalmes, whereby they were allured immediatly to forget their folly, and leaue their ſacrifice vnconſumed, ſuffering the fire to go out, and imitating vs in all our actions; they fell a lifting vp their eyes and hands to heauen as they ſaw vs do.

The 23. of Iuly they tooke a ſorrowfull farewell of vs, but being loath to leaue vs, they preſently ranne to the tops of the hils to keepe vs in their ſight as long as they could, making fires before and behind, and on each ſide of them, burning therein (as is to be ſuppoſed) ſacrifices at our departure.

Not farre without this harborough did lye certaine Ilands (we called them the Ilands of Saint *Iames*) hauing on them plentifull

tifull and great store of Seales and birds, with one of which wee
fell Iuly 24.whereon we found such prouision as might compe-
tently serue our turne for a while. We departed againe the day
next following,viz.Iuly 25.And our Generall now considering,
that the extremity of the cold not only continued but increased,
the Sunne being gone farther from vs, and that the wind blow-
ing still (as it did at first) from the Northwest,cut off all hope of
finding a passage through these Northerne parts , thought it
necessarie to loose no time; and therefore with generall consent
of all, bent his course directly to runne with the Ilands of the
Moluccas. And so hauing nothing in our view but aire and sea,
without fight of any land for the space of full 68. dayes together, wee continued our course through the maine Ocean, till
September 30. following,on which day we fell in kenne of certaine Ilands, lying about eight degrees to the Northward of
the line.

From these Ilands presently vpon the discouery of vs , came
a great number of canowes, hauing each of them in some
foure, in some sixe, in some fourteene or fifteene men,bringing
with them Coquos, fish, Potatos, and certaine fruites to small
purpose.

Their canowes were made after the fashion,that the canowes
of all the rest of the Ilands of Moluccas for the most part are:
That is of one tree,hollowed within with great art and cunning,
being made so smooth both within and without, that they bore
a glosse, as if it were a harnesse most finely burnished: A prowe
and sterne they had of one fashion , yeelding inward in manner
of a semicircle, of a great height , and hanged full of certaine
white and glistering shels for brauery: On each side of their canows,lay out two peeces of timber about a yard and halfe long,
more or lesse according to the capacitie of their boate. At the
ends whereof was fastned crossewise a great cane,the vse whereof was to keepe their canowes from ouerthrowing,and that they
might be equally borne vp on each side.

The people themselues haue the neather parts of their eares
                                                        cut

cut round or circlewife, hanging downe very low vpon their cheekes, wherein they hang things of a reafonable weight: the nailes on the fingers of fome of them, were at leaft an inch long, and their teeth as blacke as pitch ; the colour whereof they vfe to renew by often eating of an herbe, with a kind of powder, which in a cane they carrie about them to the fame purpofe. The firft fort and company of thofe canowes beeing come to our fhip (which then by reafon of a fcant wind made little way) very fubtilly and againft their natures, began in peace to traffique with vs, giuing vs one thing for another very orderly , intending (as we perceiued) hereby to worke a greater mifchiefe to vs:Intreating vs by fignes moft earneftly to draw neerer towards the fhore, that they might (if poffible) make the eafier prey both of the fhip and vs. But thefe paffing away, and others continually reforting, wee were quickly able to gueffe at them what they were: For if they receiued any thing once into their hands, they would neither giue recompence nor reftitution of it, but thought what euer they could finger to bee their owne : Expecting alwayes with browes of braffe to receiue more, but would part with nothing: Yea being reiected for their bad dealing, as thofe with whom we would haue no more to do, vfing vs fo euilly, they could not be fatisfied till they had giuen the attempt to reuenge themfelues, becaufe we would not giue them whatfoeuer they would haue for nothing: And hauing ftones good ftore in their canowes, let flie a maine of them againft vs. It was farre from our Generals meaning to requite their malice by like iniurie. Yet that they might know that he had power to doe them harme (if he had lifted) he caufed a great peece to be fhot off, not to hurt them but to affright them. Which wrought the defired effect amongft them , for at the noife thereof, they euery one leaped out of his canow into the water, and diuing vnder the keele of their boates, ftaied them from going any way till our fhip was gone a good way from them. Then they all lightly recouered into their canowes , and got them with fpeed toward the fhoare.

Notwith-

Notwithstanding other new companies (but all of the same mind) continually made resort vnto vs. And seeing that there was no good to be got by violence, they put on a shew of seeming honestie, and offering in shew to deale with vs by way of exchange; vnder that pretence they cunningly fell a filching of what they could, and one of them puld a dagger and kniues from one of our mens girdles, and being required to restore it againe, he rather vsed what meanes he could to catch at more. Neither could we at all be to ridde of this vngracious company, till we made some of them feele some smart as well as terror: and so we left that place by all passengers to bee knowne hereafter by the name of the *Island of Theeues.*

Octob.3.   Till the third of October wee could not get cleare of these consorts, but from thence we continued our course without
Octob. 16.   sight of land till the 16. of the same moneth, when we fell with foure Ilands standing in 7. deg. 5. min. to the Northward of the
Octob. 21.   line. We coasted them till the 21. day, and then anchored and watered vpon the biggest of them called Mindanao. The 22. of
Octob.22.   October as we past betweene two Ilands, about sixe or eight leagues South of Mindanao, there came from them two canows to haue talked with vs, and we would willingly haue talked with them, but there arose so much wind that put vs from them to
Octob.25.   the Southwards. October 25. we passed by the Iland named *Talao* in 3. deg. 40. min. we saw to the Northward of it three or
Octob. 30.   foure other Ilands, *Teda, Selan Saran,* (three Ilands so named to vs by an Indian) the middle whereof stands in 3. deg. we past
Nouemb.1.   the last saue one of these, & the first day of the following moneth in like manner, we past the Ile *Suaro* in 1. deg. 30. min. and the
Nou. 3.   third of Nouember wee came in sight of the Ilands of the Moluccaes as we desired.

These are foure high piked Ilands, their names, *Tirenáte, Tidóre, Matchan, Batchan,* all of them very fruitfull, and yeelding abundance of cloues, whereof wee furnished our selues of as much as we desired at a very cheape rate. At the East of them lyes a very great Iland called *Gillola.*

We

We directed our course to haue gone to _Tidore,_ but in coasting along a little Iland belonging to the king of _Terenate,_ Nouemb. 4. his deputy or Viceroy with all expedition came off to our ship in a canow, and without any feare or doubting of our good meaning came presently aboard. Who after some conference with our Generall, intreated him by any meanes to runne with _Terenate,_ not with _Tidore,_ assuring him that his king would be wondrous glad of his comming, and be ready to do for him what he could, and what our Generall in reason should require: For which purpose he himselfe would that night bee with his king to carry him the newes: with whom if he once dealt, he should find, that as he was a king so his word should stand, wheras if he dealt with the Portingals (who had the command of _Tidore_) he should find in them nothing but deceit and treachery. And besides that if he went to _Tidore_ before he came to _Terenate,_ than would his king haue nothing to doe with vs, for he held the Portingall as an enemy. On these perswasions our Generall resolued to runne with _Terenate,_ where the next day very early in the morning we came to anchor: And presently, our Generall sent a messenger to the king with a veluet cloake, for a present and token that his comming should be in peace: and that he required no other thing at his hands, but that (his victuals being spent in so long a voiage) he might haue supply from him by way of traffique and exchange of marchandise (whereof he had store of diuers sorts) of such things as he wanted. Which he thought he might be the bolder to require at his hands, both for that the thing was lawfull, and that he offered him no preiudice or wrong therein, as also becaufe he was intreated to repaire to that place by his Viceroy at Mutir, who assured him of necessarie prouision in such manner as now he required the same.

Before this, the Viceroy according to his promise had beene with the king, signifying vnto him what a mighty Prince and kingdome we belonged vnto, what good things the king might receiue from vs, not onely now, but for hereafter by way of

traffique:

traffique: yea what honour and benefit it might be to him, to be in league and friendfhip with fo noble and famous a Prince as we ferued: And farther what a difcouragement it would be to the Portugals his enemies to heare and fee it: In hearing whereof the king was fo prefently moued to the well liking of the matter, that before our meffenger could come halfe the way, he had fent the Viceroy with diuers others of his Nobles and Coun-cellors to our Generall, with fpeciall meffage that he fhould not onely haue what things he needed, or would require with peace and friendfhip, but that he would willingly entertaine amitie with fo famous and renowned a Princes as was ours, and that if it feemed good in her eyes to accept of it, he would fequefter the commodities and traffique of his whole Iland from others, efpecially from his enemies the Portugals (from whom he had nothing but by the fword) and referue it to the intercourfe of our Nation, if we would embrace it: In token whereof he had now fent to our Generall his fignet, and would within fhort time after, come in his owne perfon with his brethren and Nobles with boats or canowes into our fhip, and be a meanes of bring-ing her into a fafer harbour.

While they were deliuering their meffage to vs, our meffen-ger was come vnto the Court, who being met by the way by certaine noble perfonages, was with great folemnitie conueied into the kings prefence: at whofe hands he was moft friendly and gracioufly entertained, and hauing deliuered his errand to-gether with his prefent vnto the king, the king feemed to him to iudge himfelfe blame-worthy, that he had not fooner hafted in perfon to prefent himfelfe to our Generall, who came fo farre and from fo great a Prince; And prefently with all expedition, he made ready himfelfe with the chiefeft of all his States and Councellors to make repaire vnto vs.

The manner of his comming as it was princely, fo truly it fee-med to vs very ftrange & maruellous: feruing at the prefent not fo much to fet out his owne royall and kingly ftate (which was great) as to do honour to her highneffe to whom we belonged;

wherein

wherein how willingly he imployed himfelfe, the fequell will make manifeft.

First therefore, before his comming, did he fend off 3. great and large Canowes; in each whereof, were certaine of the greateft perfonages that were about him, attired all of them in white Lawne, or cloth of Calecut, hauing buer their heads, from one end of the Canow to the other, a couering of thinne and fine mats, borne vp by a frame made of reedes, vnder which euery man fate in order according to his dignity; the hoary heads of many of them, fet forth the greater reuerence due to their perfons, and manifeftly fhewed, that the king vfed the aduice of a graue and prudent Counfell, in his affaires. Befides thefe, were diuerfe others, young and comely men, a great number attired in white as were the other, but with manifeft differences: hauing their places alfo vnder the fame couering, but in inferior order, as their calling required.

The reft of the men were fouldiers, who ftood in comely order round about on both fides; on the outfide of whom, againe did fit the rowers in certaine galleries, which being 3. on each fide all alongft the Canow, did lie off from the fide thereof, fome 3. or 4. yards, one being orderly builded lower then the other: in euery of which galleries was an equall number of banckes, whereon did fit the rowers, about the number of fourefcoure in one Canow: In the forepart of each Canow, fate two men, the one holding a Tabret, the other a piece of braffe, whereon they both at once ftroke; and obferuing a due time and reafonable fpace betweene each ftroake, by the found thereof, directed the rowers to keepe their ftroake with their oares; as on the contrary, the rowers ending their ftroake with a fong, gaue warning to the others to ftrike againe; and fo continued they their way with maruelous fwiftneffe: neither were their Canowes naked or vnfurnifhed of warlike munition, they had each of thē, at leaft one fmall caft piece of about a yard in length mounted vpon a ftocke, which was fet vpright; befides euery man except the rowers, had his fword, dagger, and target, and

fome

ſome of them ſome other weapons, as, lances, calliuers, bowes, arrowes, and many darts.

Theſe Canowes comming neere our 'ſhip in order, rowed round about vs one after another ; and the men as they paſſe by vs, did vs a kinde of homage with great ſolemnity, the greateſt perſonages beginning firſt, with reuerend countenance and behauiour, to bow their bodies euen to the ground : which done, they put our owne meſſenger aboard vs againe, and ſignified to vs, that their king(who himſelfe was comming)had ſent them before him, to conduct our ſhip into a better roade, deſiring a halſer to be giuen them forth, that they might employ their ſeruice as their king commanded, in towing our ſhip therewith to the place aſſigned.

The king himſelfe was not farre behinde, but he alſo with 6. graue and ancient fathers in his Canow approaching, did at once together with them, yeeld vs a reuerend kinde of obeyſance in farre more humble manner, then was to be expected ; he was of a tall ſtature, very corpulent and well ſet together, of a very princely and gratious countenance ; his reſpect amongſt his owne was ſuch, that neither his Viceroy of Mutir aforenamed, nor any other of his counſellers, durſt ſpeake vnto him but vpon their knees, not riſing againe till they were licenced.

Whoſe comming as it was to our generall, no ſmall cauſe of goodliking, ſo was he receiued in the beſt manner we could, anſwerable vnto his ſtate : our ordinance thundred, which wee mixed with great ſtore of ſmall ſhot, among which ſounding our trumpets, and other inſtruments of muſick, both of ſtill and loud noiſe, wherewith he was ſo much delighted, that requeſting our muſick to come into the boate, hee ioyned his Canow to the ſame, and was towed at leaſt a whole houre together, with the boate at the ſterne of our ſhip: Beſides this, our generall ſent him ſuch preſents, as he thought, might both requite his curteſy already receiued, and worke a farther confirmation, of that goodliking and friendſhip already begunne.

The king being thus in muſicall paradiſe, and enioying that

wherewith he was fo highly pleafed; his brother named *Moro* with no leffe brauery, then any of the reft, accompanied alfo with a great number of gallant followers, made the like repaire, and gaue vs like refpect; and his homage done he fell afterne of vs, till we came to anchor: neither did our generall leaue his curtefie vnrewarded, but bountifully pleafed him alfo before we parted.

The king as foone as we were come to anchor, craued pardon to be gone, and fo tooke leaue, promifing vs, that the next day he would come aboard, and in the meane time would prepare and fend fuch victualls, as were requifite and neceffary for our prouifion.

Accordingly the fame night, and the morrow following, we receiued what was there to be had, by way of traffique, to wit, rice in pretty quantity, hennes, fugar canes, imperfect and liquid fugar, a fruit which they call *Figo(Magellane* calls it a figge of a fpan long, but is no other then that which the Spaniards and Portingalls haue named *Plantanes)Cocoes* and a kind of meale which they call *Sago*, made of the toppes of certaine trees, tafting in the mouth like foure curdes, but meltes away like fugar; whereof they make a kinde of cake which will keepe good at leaft 10. yeares; of this laft we made the greateft quantity of our prouifion: for a few cloues wee did alfo traffique, whereof for a fmall matter, wee might haue had greater ftore, then we could well tell where to beftow: but our generalls care was, that the fhip fhould not be too much peftered or annoyed therewith.

At the time appointed, our generall(hauing fet all things in order to receiue him) looked for the kings returne, who failing both in time and promife, fent his brother to make his excufe, and to intreat our generall to come on fhoare; his brother being the while to remaine aboard, as a pawne for his fafe reftoring: our generall could willingly haue confented, if the king himfelfe had not firft broke his word: the confideration whereof, bred an vtter difliking in the whole company, who by no

meanes

meanes would giue confent, he fhould hazard himfelfe, efpecially, for that the kings brother had vttered certaine words, in
fecret conference with our generall aboard his cabbin, which
bred no fmall fufpition of ill intent; our generall being thus refolued not to goe afhoare at that time, referued the Viceroy for
a pledge, and fo fent certaine of his gentlemen to the court,
both to accompany the kings brother, and alfo with fpeciall
meffage to the king himfelfe.

They being come fomewhat neere vnto the caftle, were receiued by another brother of the kings, and certaine others of
the greateft ftates, and conducted with great honour towards
the caftle, where being brought into a large and faire houfe,
they faw gathered together a great multitude of people, by fup-
pofition at leaft 1000. the chiefe whereof, were placed round a-
bout the houfe, according as it feemed to their degrees and calling, the reft remained without.

The houfe was in forme foure fquare, couered all ouer with
cloth of diuerfe colours, not much vnlike our vfuall pentadoes
borne vpon a frame of reedes, the fides being open from the
groundfell to the couering, and furnifhed with feates round a-
bout: it feemes it was there councell-houfe and not commonly
employed to any other vfe.

At the fide of this houfe, next vnto the caftle was feated the
chaire of ftate, hauing directly ouer it, and extending very largely euery way, a very faire and rich canopy, as the ground alfo
for fome 10. or 12. pafes compaffe, was couered with cloth
of Arras.

Whileft our gentlemen attended in this place the comming
of the king, which was about the fpace of halfe an houre, they
had the better opportunity to obferue thefe things; as alfo that
before the kings comming, there were already fet threefcore noble graue and ancient perfonages, all of them reported to be of
the kings priuy Councell: at the neather end of the houfe were
placed a great company of yong men, of comely perfonage and
attire. With out the houfe on the right fide, ftood foure ancient
comely

comely hoare-headed men , cloathed all in red downe to the
ground, but attired on their heads not much vnlike the Turkes;
thefe they called Romans,or ftrangers, who lay as lidgiers there
to keepe continuall traffique with this people : there were alfo
two Turkes one Italian as lidgiers : and laft of all one Spaniard,
who being freed by the kings out of the hands of the Portugals,
in the recouering of the Iland, ferued him now in ftead of a
fouldier.

The king at laft comming from the caftle, with 8. or 10. more
graue Senators following him, had a very rich canopy(adorned
in the middeft with embofsings of gold)borne ouer him, and
was garded with 12. lances the points turned downeward: our
men (accompanied with *Moro* the kings brother) arofe to meet
him, and he very gratioufly did welcome and entertaine them.

He was for perfon, fuch as we haue before defcribed him, of
lowe voice, temperate in fpeech, of kingly demeanour, and a
Moore by nation. His attire was after the fafhion of the reft of
his countrey, but farre more fumptuous, as his condition and
ftate required: from the waft to the ground, was all cloth of
gold, and that very rich; his legges bare, but on his feet a paire
of fhooes of cordiuant died red : in the attire of his head, were
finely wreathed in diuerfe rings of plated gold, of an inch, or an
inch and halfe in breadth,which made a faire and princely fhew,
fomewhat refembling a crowne in forme ; about his necke hee
had a chaine of perfect gold, the linkes very great and onefold
double; on his left hand was a Diamond, an Emerald, a Ruby,
and a Turky,4,very faire and perfect jewells, on his right hand
in one ring, a big and perfect Turky , and in another ring many
Diamonds of a fmaller fize, very artificially fet and couched
together.

As thus he fate in his chaire of State , at his right fide there
ftood a page with a very coftly fanne(richly embrodered and be-
fet with Saphires)breathing & gathering the aire to refrefh the
king, the place being very hot, both by reafon of the funne, and
the affembly of fo great a multitude. After a while our gentlemen

men hauing deliuered their meffage, and receiued anfwer, were licenced to depart, and were fafely conducted backe againe, by one of the chiefe of the kings Councell who had charge from the king himfelfe to performe the fame.

Our gentlemen obferuing the caftle as well as they could, could not conceiue it to be a place of any great force: two onely canons they there faw, and thofe at that prefent vntrauerfable becaufe vnmounted. Thefe with all other furniture of like fort which they haue, they haue gotten them from the Portingals, by whom the caftle it felfe was alfo builded, whiles they inhabited that place and Iland. Who feeking to fettle a tyrannous gouern-ment (as in other places fo) ouer this people, and not conten-ting themfelues with a better eftate then they deferued (except they might (as they thought) make fure worke by leauing none of the royall bloud aliue, who fhould make challenge to the kingdome) cruelly murthered the king himfelfe (father to him who now raignes) and intended the like to all his fonnes. Which cruelty inftead of eftablifhing, brought fuch a fhaking on their vfurped eftate, that they were faine, without couenanting to car-rie away goods, munition, or any thing elfe to quitte the place and the whole Iland to faue their liues.

For the prefent king with his brethren in reuenge of their fa-thers murther, fo beftirred themfelues, that the Portingall was wholly driuen from that Iland, and glad that he yet keepes foo-ting in *Tidore*. Thefe foure yeares this king hath beene increa-fing, and was (as was affirmed) at that prefent, Lord of an hun-dred Ilands thereabout; and was euen now preparing his forces to hazard a chance with the Portingals for *Tidore* it felfe.

The people are Moores, whofe Religion confifts much in cer-taine fuperftitious obferuations of new Moones, and certaine feafons, with a rigid and ftrickt kind of fafting. We had experi-ence hereof in the Viceroy and his retinue, who lay aboard vs all the time for the moft part during our abode in this place : who during their prefcribed time, would neither eate nor drinke, not fo much as a cup of cold water in the day (fo zealous are they in their felfe deuifed worfhip) but yet in the night would eate three times, and that very largely. This *Terenate* ftands in 27. min. North latitude.

While we rode at anchor in the harbour at *Terenate*, befides the natiues there came aboard vs another, a goodly gentleman, very well accompanied with his interpreter, to view our fhip, and to conferre with our Generall : he was apparelled much after our manner, moft neate and Courtlike: his carriage the moft refpectiue, and full of difcreet behauiour that euer we had feene; Hee told vs that he was himfelfe but a ftranger in thofe Ilands, being a naturall of the Prouince of *Paghia* in *China* ; his name, *Panfaos* of the familie of *Hombu* : of which familie there had 11. raigned in continuall fucceffion thefe two hundred yeares, and king *Bonog* by the death of his elder brother (who dyed by a fall from his horfe) the rightfull heire of all *China*, is the twelfth of this race:he is of 22. yeares of age: his mother yet liuing:he hath a wife, and by her one fonne: he is well beloued, and highly honoured of all his fubiects, and liues in great peace from any feare of forreine inuafion : but it was not this mans fortune to enioy his part of this happineffe both of his king and countrey, as hee moft defired.

For being accufed of a capitall crime whereof (though free) yet he could not euidently make his innocency appeare, and knowing the peremptory iuftice of *China*, to be irreuocable, if he fhould expect the fentence of the Iudges; he before hand made fuite to his king, that it would pleafe him to commit his trial to Gods prouidence and iudgement, and to that end to permit him to trauell on this condition, that if he brought not home fome worthy intelligence, fuch as his Maieftie had neuer had before, and were moft fit to be knowne, and moft honorable for *China*, he fhould for euer liue an exile, or elfe dye for daring to fet foot againe in his owne countrey: for he was affured that the God of heauen had care of innocency.

The king granted his fuite, and now he had beene three yeares abroad, and at this prefent came from *Tidore* (where he had remained

N

mained

mained two moneths) to ſee the Engliſh Generall, of whom he heard ſuch ſtrange things, and from him (if it pleaſed God to afford it) to learne ſome ſuch intelligence as might make way for his returne into his countrey: and therefore he earneſtly intreated our Generall, to make relation to him of the occaſion, way, and manner of his comming ſo far from England thither, with the manifold occurrences that had happened to him by the way.

Our Generall gaue ample ſatisfaction to each part of his requeſt: the ſtranger hearkened with great attention and delight to his diſcourſe, and as he naturally excelled in memory (beſides his helpe of art to better the ſame) ſo he firmely printed it in his mind, and with great reuerence thanked God, who had ſo vnexpectedly brought him, to the notice of ſuch admirable things. Then fell he to intreate our Generall with many moſt earneſt and vehement perſuaſions, that he would be content to ſee his countrey before his departure any farther Weſtward, that it ſhould be a moſt pleaſant, moſt honourable, and moſt profitable thing for him that he ſhould gaine hereby the notice, and carrie home the deſcription of one of the moſt ancient, mightieſt and richeſt kingdomes in the world. Hereupon he tooke occaſion to relate the number and greatneſſe of the Prouinces, with the rare commodities and good things they yeelded: the number, ſtatelineſſe, and riches of their Cities, with what abundance of men, victuals, munition, and all manner of neceſſaries and delightfull things they were ſtored with: In particular, touching ordnance and great gunnes (the late inuention of a ſcab-ſhind Frier amongſt vs in Europe) he related that in *Suntien* (by ſome called *Quinzai*) which is the chiefeſt Citie of all *China*, they had braſſe ordnance of all ſorts (much eaſier to be trauerſed then ours were, and ſo perfectly made that they would hit a ſhilling) aboue 2000. yeares agoe. With many other worthy things which our Generals owne experience (if it would pleaſe him to make triall) would (better then his relation) aſſure him of. The brize would ſhortly ſerue very fitly to carrie him thither, and he

himſelfe

himselfe would accompanie him all the way. Hé accounted himselfe a happie man, that he had but seene and spoken with vs; the relation of it might perhaps serue him to recouer fauour in his countrey : but if he could preuaile with our Generall himselfe to go thither, he doubted not but it would be a meanes of his great aduancement, and increase of honour with his king: Notwithstanding our Generall could not on such persuasions be induced, and so the stranger parted sorrie, that he could not preuaile in his request, yet exceeding glad of the intelligence he had learned.

By the ninth of Nouember hauing gotten what prouision the place could affoord vs, wee then set sayle : and considering that our ship for want of trimming was now growne foule, that our caske and vessels for water were much decayed; and that diuers other things stood in need of reparation:our next care was, how wee might fall with such a place where with safetie we might a while stay for the redressing of these inconueniences. The calmenesse of the winds, which are almost continuall before the comming of the brize (which was not yet expected) perswaded vs it was the fittest time that we could take.

With this resolution wee sayled along till Nouember 14. at what time we arriued at a little Iland (to the Southward of *Celébes*) standing in 1. deg. 40. min. towards the pole antarticke: which being without inhabitants, gaue vs the better hope of quiet abode. We anchored and finding the place conuenient for our purposes (there wanting nothing here which we stood in need of, but onely water which wee were faine to fetch from another Iland somewhat farther to the South) made our abode here for 26. whole dayes together.

The first thing we did, we pitched our tents and intrenched our selues as strongly as we could vpon the shoare, lest at any time perhaps we might haue beene disturbed by the inhabitants of the greater Iland which lay not farre to the Westward of vs; after we had prouided thus for our security, wee landed our goods, and had a Smiths forge set vp, both for the making of

N 2　　　　　　　　　some

some neceſſarie ſhipworke, and for the repairing of ſome iron-hooped caskes, without which they could not long haue ſerued our vſe: and for that our Smiths coales were all ſpent long before this time; there was order giuen and followed for the burning of charcoale, by which that want might be ſupplyed.

We trimd our ſhip, and performed our other buſineſſes to our content. The place affording vs not onely all neceſſaries (which we had not of our owne before) thereunto, but alſo wonderfull refreſhing to our wearied bodies, by the comfortable reliefe and excellent prouiſion that here we found, whereby of ſickely, weake, and decayed (as many of vs ſeemed to be before our comming hither) we in ſhort ſpace grew all of vs to be ſtrong, luſty, and healthfull perſons. Beſides this, we had rare experience of Gods wonderfull wiſedome in many rare and admirable creatures which here we ſaw.

The whole Iland is a through growne wood, the trees for the moſt part are of large and high ſtature, very ſtraight and cleane without bowes, ſaue onely in the very top. The leaues whereof are not much vnlike our broomes in England: Among theſe trees, night by night did ſhew themſelues an infinite ſwarme of fierie-ſeeming-wormes flying in the aire, whoſe bodies (no bigger then an ordinary flie) did make a ſhew, and giue ſuch light as if euery twigge on euery tree had beene a lighted candle: or as if that place had beene the ſtarry ſphearе. To theſe wee may adde the relation of another, almoſt as ſtrange a creature, which here we ſaw, and that was an innumerable multitude of huge Bats or reare-mice, equalling or rather exceeding a good Henne in bigneſſe. They flie with maruellous ſwiftneſſe, but their flight is very ſhort; and when they light, they hang onely by the bowes with their backes downeward.

Neither may wee without ingratitude (by reaſon of the ſpeciall vſe we made of them) omit to ſpeake of the huge multitude, of a certaine kinde of Crayfiſh, of ſuch a ſize, that one was ſufficient to ſatisfie foure hungry men at a dinner, being a very good and reſtoratiue meate; the eſpeciall meane (as we conceiued it) of our increaſe of health.   They

They are as farre as we could perceiue, vtter ſtrangers to the ſea, liuing alwayes on the land, where they worke themſelues earths, as do the conies, or rather they dig great and huge caues, vnder the rootes of the moſt huge and monſtrous trees, where they lodge themſelues by companies together. Of the ſame ſort and kind, we found in other places, about the Iland *Celebes* ſome that for want of other refuge, when we came to take them, did clime vp into trees to hide themſelues, whether we were enforced to clime after them, if we would haue them, which wee would not ſticke to do rather then to be without them : this Iland we called *Crab-iland.*

All neceſſary cauſes of our ſtaying longer in this place being at laſt finiſhed, our generall prepared to be in a readineſſe, to take the firſt aduantage of the comming of the brize or winde which we expected ; and hauing the day before, furniſhed our ſelues with freſh water from the other Iland, and taken in prouiſion of wood and the like : December 12. we put to ſea, directing our courſe toward the Weſt : the 16. day wee had ſight of the Iland *Celebes* or *Silébis,* but hauing a bad winde, and being intangled among many Ilands, incumbred alſo with many other difficulties, and ſome dangers, & at laſt meeting with a deep bay, out of which we could not in three daies turne out againe, wee could not by any meanes recouer the North of *Silébis,* or continue on our courſe farther Weſt, but were inforced to alter the ſame toward the South ; finding that courſe alſo to be both difficult and very dangerous, by reaſon of many ſhoales, which lay farre off, here and there among the Ilands, inſomuch, that in all our paſſages from England hitherto, we had neuer more care to keepe our ſelues afloate, and from ſticking on them : thus were we forced to beate vp and downe with extraordinary care and circumſpection till Ianuary 9. at which time, we ſuppoſed that we had at laſt attained a free paſſage, the land turning euidently in our ſight about to Weſtward, and the wind being enlarged, followed vs as we deſired with a reaſonable gale.

When loe on a ſudden, when we leaſt ſuſpected no ſhew or

1579.

Dec. 12.
Dec. 16.

Ian. 9.

N 3 ſuſpition

suspition of danger appearing to vs, and we were now sailing onward with full sailes, in the beginning of the first watch of the said day at night, euen in a moment our ship was laid vp fast vpon a desperate shoale, with no other likelihood in appearance, but that wee with her must there presently perish : there being no probability how any thing could be saued, or any person scape aliue.

The vnexpectednesse of so extreame a danger, presently roused vs vp to looke about vs, but the more we looked, the lesse hope we had of getting cleere of it againe, so that nothing now presenting it selfe to our mindes, but the ghastly appearance of instant death, affording no respit or time of pausing, called vpon vs to turne our thoughts another way, to renounce the world to deny our selues, and to commend our selues into the mercifull hands of our most gratious God : to this purpose wee presently fell prostrate, and with ioyned prayers sent vp vnto the throne of grace, humbly besought almighty God, to extend his mercy vnto vs in his sonne *Chrift Iesus*; and so preparing as it were our necks vnto the blocke, we euery minute expected the finall stroake to be giuen vnto vs.

Notwithstanding that we expected nothing but imminent death, yet (that we might not seeme to tempt God, by leauing any second meanes vnattempted which he afforded) presently as soone as prayers were ended, our generall (exhorting vs to haue the especiallest care of the better part, to wit, the soule, and adding many comfortable speeches, of the ioyes of that other life, which wee now alone looked for) incouraged vs all to bestirre our selues, shewing vs the way thereto by his owne example; and first of all the pump being well plyed, and the ship freed of water, we found our leakes to be nothing increased, which though it gaue vs no hope of deliuerance, yet it gaue vs some hope of respit, insomuch, as it assured vs that the bulke was found, which truly we acknowledged to be an immediate prouidence of God alone, insomuch, as no strength of wood and iron could haue possibly borne so hard and violent a shocke, as our

ship

ship did, dashing herselfe vnder full saile against the rockes, except the extraordinary hand of God, had supported the same.

Our next assay was for good ground and anchor-hold, to seaward of vs (whereon to hale) by which meanes if by any, our generall put vs in comfort, that there was yet left some hope to cleere our selues : in his owne person, he therefore vndertooke the charge of sounding, and but euen a boates length from the ship, he found that the bottom could not by any length of line be reached vnto : so that the beginnings of hope, which wee were willing to haue conceiued before, were by this meanes quite dasht againe ; yea our misery seemed to be increased, for whereas at first wee could looke for nothing but a present end, that expectation was now turned, into the awaiting for a lingring death, of the two, the farre more fearefull to be chosen? one thing fell out happily for vs, that the most of our men did not conceiue this thing, which had they done, they would in all likelihood haue beene so much discouraged, that their sorrow would the more disable them, to haue sought the remedy : our generall with those few others, that could iudge of the euent wisely, dissembling the same, and giuing in the meane time cheerfull speeches, and good incouragements vnto the rest.

For whiles it seemed to be a cleere case, that our ship was so fast moared, that shee could not stirr ; it necessarily followed, that either we were there to remaine on the place with her ; or else leauing her to commit our selues in a most poore and helplesse state, to seeke some other place of stay and refuge, the better of which two choices, did carry with it the appearance of worse then 1000. deathes.

As touching our ship, this was the comfort that shee could giue vs, that shee her selfe lying there confined already vpon the hard and pinching rocks, did tell vs plaine, that shee continually expected her speedy dispatch, as soone as the sea and windes should come, to be the seuere executioners of that heauy iudgement, by the appointment of the eternall iudge already

die

dy giuen vpon her, who had committed her there to Adaman-
tine bonds in a moſt narrow priſon, againſt their comming for
that purpoſe : ſo that if we would ſtay with her, we muſt pe-
riſh with her; or if any by any yet vnperceiueable meanes,
ſhould chance to be deliuered, his eſcape muſt needs be a perpetuall miſery, it being farre better to haue periſhed together,
then with the loſſe and abſence of his friends, to liue in a ſtrange
land : whether a ſolitary life (the better choice) among wild
beaſtes, as a bird on the mountaines without all comfort, or a-
mong the barbarous people of the heathen, in intollerable
bondage both of body and minde.

And put the caſe that her day of deſtruction ſhould be defer-
red, longer then either reaſon could perſwade vs, or in any likelihood could ſeeme poſſible (it being not in the power of earth-
ly things, to indure what ſhee had ſuffred already) yet could our
abode there profit vs nothing, but increaſe our wretchedneſſe,
and enlarge our ſorrows, for as her ſtore and victualls were not
much (ſufficient to ſuſtaine vs onely ſome few daies, without
hope of hauing any increaſe, no not ſo much as of a cup of cold
water) ſo muſt it ineuitably come to paſſe, that we (as children in
the mothers wombe) ſhould be driuen euen to eate the fleſh
from of our owne armes, ſhee being no longer able to ſuſtaine
vs; and how horrible a thing this would haue proued, is eaſy by
any one to be perceiued.

And whither (had we departed from her) ſhould we haue receiued any comfort; nay the very impoſſibility of going, appeared to be no leſſe, then thoſe other before mentioned : our
boate was by no meanes able at once, to carry aboue 20. perſons
with any ſafety, and we were 58. in all, the neereſt land was ſix
leagues from vs, and the winde from the ſhoare directly bent a-
gainſt vs : or ſhould we haue thought of ſetting ſome aſhoare,
and after that to haue fetched the reſt, there being no place
thereabout without inhabitants, the firſt that had landed muſt
firſt haue fallen into the hand of the enemie, and ſo the reſt in
order, and though perhaps we might eſcape the ſword, yet
would

would our life haue beene worſe then death,not alone in reſpect of our wofull captiuity, and bodily miſeries , but moſt of all in reſpect of our Chriſtian liberty,being to be depriued of all pub-lique meanes of ſeruing the true God, and continually grieued with the horrible impieties and diuelliſh idolatries of the hea-then.

Our miſerie beeing thus manifeſt , the very conſideration wherof muſt needs haue ſhaken fleſh and bloud,if faith in Gods promiſes had not mightily ſuſtained vs, we paſt the night with earneſt longings that the day would once appeare , the meane time we ſpent in often prayers,and other godly exerciſes, there-by comforting our ſelues,and refreſhing our hearts, ſtriuing to bring our ſelues to an humble ſubmiſſion vnder the hand of God, and to a referring our ſelues wholly to his good will and pleaſure.

The day therefore at length appearing, and it being almoſt full ſea about that time, after we had giuen thankes to God for his forbearing of vs hitherto , and had with teares called vpon him to bleſſe our labours; we againe renewed our trauell, to ſee if we could now poſſibly find any anchor hold, which we had formerly ſought in vaine. But this ſecond attempt proued as fruitleſſe as the former, and left vs nothing to truſt to, but pray-ers and teares, ſeeing it appeared impoſſible that euer the fore-caſt counſell,pollicie, or power of man could euer effect the de-liuery of our ſhip, except the Lord onely miraculouſly ſhould do the ſame.

It was therefore preſently motioned, and by generall voice determined to commend our caſe to God alone , leauing our ſelues wholly in his hand; to ſpill or ſaue vs as ſeeme beſt to his gracious wiſedome. And that our faith might bee the better ſtrengthened, and the comfortable apprehenſion of Gods mer-cie in Chriſt, be more clearely felt; we had a Sermon and the Sacrament of the bodie and bloud of our Sauiour celebrated.

After this ſweet repaſt was thus receiued, and other holy ex-erciſes adioyned were ended, leſt we ſhould ſeeme guilty in any respect for not vsing all lawfull meanes we could inuent; we fell to one other practise yet vnassayed, to wit, to vnloading of our ship by casting some of her goods into the sea: which thing as it was attempted most willingly, so was it dispatched in very short time. So that euen those things which we before this time, nor any other in our case could be without, did now seeme as things onely worthy to be despised, yea we were herein so forward, that neither our munition for defence, nor the very meale for sustentation of our liues could find fauour with vs, but euerie thing as it first came to hand went ouerboard: assuring our selues of this, that if it pleased God once to deliuer vs out of that most desperate strait wherein we were, he would fight for vs against our enemies, neither would he suffer vs to perish for want of bread. But when all was done, it was not any of our endeuours, but Gods onely hand that wrought our deliuerie; twas he alone that brought vs euen vnder the very stroake of death; twas he alone that said vnto vs, Returne againe ye sonnes of men; twas he alone that set vs at liberty againe, that made vs safe and free, after that we had remained in the former miserable condition, the full space of twentie houres, to his glorious name be the euerlasting praise.

The manner of our deliuery (for the relation of it will especially be expected) was onely this. The place whereon we sate so fast, was a firme rocke in a cleft, whereof it was we stucke on the larbord side, at low water there was not aboue sixe foote depth in all on the starbord, within little distance as you haue heard no bottome to be found, the brize during the whole time that we thus were stayed, blew somewhat stiffe directly against our broad side, and so perforce kept the ship vpright: It pleased God in the beginning of the tyde, while the water was yet almost at lowest, to slacke the stiffenesse of the wind; and now our ship who required thirteene foot water to make her fleet, and had not at that time on the one side aboue seuen at most, wanting her prop on the other side, which had too long alreadie kept her vp, fell a heeling towards the deepe water, and

by

by that meanes freed her keele and made vs glad men.

This shoale is at least three or foure leagues in length, it lies in 2. deg. lacking three or foure minutes South latitude. The day of this deliuerance was the tenth of Ianuary.

Of all the dangers that in our whole voyage we met with, this was the greatest, but it was not the last as may appeare by what ensueth. Neither could we indeed for a long season free our selues from the continuall care and feare of them; nor could we euer come to any conuenient anchoring, but were continually for the most part tost amongst the many Ilands and shoales (which lye in infinite number round about on the South parts of *Celébes*) till the eight day of the following moneth.

Ian. 12. being not able to beare our sayles by reason of the tempest and fearing of the dangers, we let fall our anchors vpon a shoale in 3. deg. 30. min. Ian. 14. we were gotten a little farther South, where at an Iland in 4. deg. 6. min. we againe cast anchor and spent a day in watering and wooding. After this wee met with foule weather, Westerly winds, and dangerous shoales for many dayes together: insomuch that we were vtterly weary of this coast of *Sillebis*, and thought best to beare with *Timor*. The Southermost cape of *Sillebis* stands in 5. deg. that side the line.

But of this coast of *Sillebis* we could not so easily cleare our selues. The 20. of Ianua. wee were forced to runne with a small Iland not farre from thence; where hauing sent our boate a good distance from vs to search out a place where we might anchor: wee were suddenly enuironed with no small extremities, for there arose a most violent, yea an intollerable flaw and storme out of the Southwest against vs, making vs (who were on a lee shoare amongst most dangerous and hidden shoales) to feare extreamely not onely the losse of our boate and men, but the present losse of our selues, our ship and goods, or the casting of those men whom God should spare into the hands of Infidels. Which misery could not by any power or industry of ours haue beene auoided, if the mercifull goodnesse of God had not (by staying the outragious extremities wherewith we were set

vpon)

vpon) wrought our preſent deliuery, by whoſe vnſpeakeable mercy our men and boate alſo were vnexpectedly, yet ſafely, reſtored vnto vs.

Wee gate off from this place as well as we could, and continued on our courſe till the 26. day, when the winde tooke vs, very ſtrong againſt vs, Weſt and Weſt Southweſt, ſo as that wee could beare no more ſaile, till the end of that moneth was full expired.

February 1. we ſaw very high land, and as it ſeemed well inhabited, we would faine haue borne with it to haue got ſome ſuccour, but the weather was ſo ill, that we could finde no harbour, and we were very fearefull of aduenturing our ſelues too farre, amongſt the many dangers which were neere the ſhoare. The third day alſo we ſaw a little Iland, but being vnable to beare any ſaile, but onely to ly at hull, we were by the ſtorme carried away, and could not fetch it. February 6. we ſaw fiue Ilands, one of them towards the Eaſt, and foure towards the Weſt of vs, one bigger then another, at the biggeſt of which we caſt anchor, and the next day watred and wooded.

After we had gone hence on February 8. we deſcried two canowes, who hauing deſcried vs as it ſeemes before, came willingly vnto vs, and talked with vs, alluring and conducting vs to their towne not farre off, named *Baratiua*, it ſtands in 7. deg. 13. min. South the line.

The people are Gentiles of handſome body, and comely ſtature, of ciuill demeanour, very iuſt in dealing, and courteous to ſtrangers, of all which we had euident proofe, they ſhewing themſelues moſt glad of our coming and cheerfully ready to relieue our wants, with whatſoeuer their country could afford. The men goe all naked ſaue their heads and ſecret parts, euery one hauing one thing or other hanging at his eares. Their women are couered from the middle to the foote, wearing vpon their naked armes bracelets, and that in no ſmall number, ſome hauing nine at leaſt vpon each arme, made for the moſt part of horne or braſſe, whereof the lighteſt (by our eſtimation) would weigh 2. ounces.
                                                                    VVith

With this people linnen cloth (whereof they make roles for their heads, and girdles to weare about their loynes) is the beſt marchandiſe and of greateſt eſtimation: They are alſo much delighted with Margaretas (which in their language they call Saleta) and ſuch other like trifles.

Their Iland is both rich and fruitfull, rich in gold, ſiluer, copper, tinne, ſulpher, &c. neither are they onely expert to try thoſe mettalls, but very skillfull alſo in working of them artificially, into diuerſe formes and ſhapes, as pleaſeth them beſt. Their fruites are diuerſe likewiſe and plentifull, as, nutmegges, ginger, long pepper, limons, cucumbers, cocoes, figoes, ſagu, with diuerſe other ſorts, whereof we had one in reaſonable quantity, in bigneſſe forme and huske, much like a bay-berry, hard in ſubſtance, but pleaſant in taſt, which being ſod becommeth ſoft, and is a moſt profitable and nouriſhing meate : of each of theſe wee receiued of them, whatſoeuer wee deſired for our need; inſomuch that (ſuch was Gods gratious goodneſſe to vs) the old prouerbe was verified with vs, *After a ſtorme commeth a calme, after warre peace, after ſcarcity followeth plenty*; ſo that in all our voyage (*Terenate* onely excepted) from our departure out of our owne countrey hitherto, wee found not any where greater comfort and refreſhing, then we did at this time in this place; in refreſhing and furniſhing our ſelues, here we ſpent 2. dayes, and departed hence February 10.

When we were come into the height of 8. deg. 4. min. Feb. 12. in the morning we eſpied a greene Iland to the Southward; not long after, two other Ilands on the ſame ſide, and a great one more towards the North: they ſeemed all to be well inhabited, but wee had neither need nor deſire to goe to viſit them, and ſo we paſt by them. The 14. day wee ſaw ſome other reaſonable bigge Ilands, and February 16. we paſt betweene foure or fiue bigge Ilands more which lay in the height 9. deg. 40. min.

The 18. we caſt anchor vnder a little Iland, whence we departed againe the day following; we wooded here, but other reliefe except two turtles we receiued none.

O 3

The

1579.
Febr.22. The 22.day we loſt ſight of three Ilands on our ſtarboard ſide, which lay in 10. deg. and ſome odde minutes.

After this, we paſt on to the Weſtward without ſtay or any thing to be taken notice of, till the 9. of March when in the mor-
March 9. ning wee eſpied land, ſome part thereof very high in 8.de.20.m. South latitude : here we anchored that night, and the next day
March 10. weighed againe, and bearing farther North, and neerer the ſhoare, we came to anchor the ſecond time.

March 11. The eleuenth of March we firſt tooke in water, and after ſent
March 12. our boate againe to ſhoare, where we had traffique with the people of the country ; whereupon the ſame day, we brought our ſhip more neere the towne : and hauing ſetled our ſelues there that night, the next day our generall ſent his man aſhoare, to preſent the king with certaine cloth, both linnen and wool-len, beſides ſome ſilkes, which hee gladly and thankfully recei-ued, and returned rice, cocoes, hennes, and other victualls in way of recompence. This Iland we found to be the Iland *Iaua*, the middle whereof ſtands in 7. deg. and 30. min. beyond the equator.

March 13. The 13.of March our general himſelf with many of his gen-tlemen, and others went to ſhoare, and preſented the king (of whom he was ioyfully and louingly receiued) with his muſicke, and ſhewed him the manner of our vſe of armes, by training his men with their pikes & other weapons, which they had before him : for the preſent we were entertained as we deſired, and at laſt diſmiſſed with a promiſe of more victuals to bee ſhortly ſent vs.

In this Iland there is one chiefe, but many vnder-gouernors, or petty kings,whom they call *Raias*, who liue in great familia-
March 14. ritie and friendſhip one with another. The 14.day we receiued
March 15. victuals from two of them, and the day after that, to wit,the 15. three of theſe kings in their owne perſons came aboard to ſee our Generall, and to view our ſhip and warlike munition. They were well pleaſed with what they ſaw, and with the entertaine-ment which we gaue them. And after theſe had beene with vs,
and

and on their returne had as it seemes related what they found, *Raia Donan* the chiefe king of the whole land bringing victuals with him for our reliefe: he also the next day after came aboard vs. Few were the dayes that one or more of these kings did misse to visit vs, insomuch that we grew acquainted with the names of many of them, as of *Raia Pataiára*, *Raia Cabocapálla*, *Raia Mangbángo*, *Raia Bocabarra*, *Raia Timbánton*: whom our Generall alwayes entertained with the best cheere that wee could make, and shewed them all the commodities of our ship, with our ordnance and other armes and weapons, and the seuerall furnitures belonging to each, and the vses for which they serued. His musicke also and all things else whereby he might do them pleasure, wherein they tooke exceeding great delight with admiration.

March 21.

One day amongst the rest, viz. March 21. *Raia Donan* comming aboard vs, in requitall of our musick which was made to him, presented our generall with his country musick, which though it were of a very strange kind, yet the sound was pleasant and delightfull: the same day, he caused an oxe also to be brought to the waters side, and deliuered to vs, for which he was to his content rewarded by our Generall, with diuerse sorts of very costly silks which he held in great esteeme.

Though our often giuing entertainement in this manner, did hinder vs much in the speedy dispatching of our businesses, and made vs spend the more dayes about them, yet here we found all such conuenient helpes, that to our contents we at last ended them: the matter of greatest importance which we did (besides victualing) was the new trimming and washing of our ship, which by reason of our long voyage was so ouergrowne with a kind of shell-fish sticking fast vnto her, that it hindred her exceedingly, and was a great trouble to her sayling.

The people (as are their kings) are a louing, a very true, and a iust dealing people. We traffiqued with them for hens, goats, cocoes, plantons, and other kinds of victuals, which they offered vs in such plenty that we might haue laden our ship if we had needed. We

1580.
March 26. We tooke our leaues and departed from them the 26. of March, and set our course West South West, directly towards the cape of good hope, or *Bon Esperance*, and continued without touch of ought, but aire and water, till the 21. of May, when we

May 21. espied land (to wit a part of the maine of *Africa*) in some places very high, vnder the latitude of 31. deg. and halfe.

Iune 15. Wee coasted along till Iune 15. on which day, hauing very faire weather, and the winde at Southeast, wee past the cape it-selfe so neere in sight, that we had beene able with our pieces to haue shot to land.

Iuly 15. Iuly 15. we fell with the land againe about *Rio de Sesto*, where we saw many negroes in their boates a fishing, whereof 2. came very neere vs, but we cared not to stay, nor had any talke or dea-ling with them.

Iuly 22. The 22. of the same moneth, wee came to *Sierra Leona*, and spent two dayes for watering in the mouth of *Tagoine*, and then

Iuly 24. put to sea againe; here also we had oisters, and plenty of lem-mons, which gaue vs good refreshing.

August 15.
Aug. 16. We found our selues vnder the Tropick of *Cancer* August 15. hauing the winde at Northeast, and we 50. leagues off from the neerest land.

Sept. 26. The 22. day we were in the height of the Canaries.

And the 26. of Sept. (which was Monday in the iust and ordi-nary reckoning of those that had stayed at home in one place or countrie, but in our computation was the Lords day or Sonday) we safely with ioyfull minds and thankfull hearts to God, arriued at Plimoth, the place of our first setting forth after we had spent 2. yeares 10. moneths and some few odde daies beside, in seeing the wonders of the Lord in the deep, in discouering so many ad-mirable things, in going through with so many strange aduen-tures, in escaping out of so many dangers, and ouercomming so many difficulties in this our encompassing of this neather globe, and passing round about the world, which we haue related.

Soli rerum maximarum Effectori,
Soli totius mundi Gubernatori,
Soli suorum Conseruatori,
Soli Deo sit semper Gloria.
FINIS.